Alchemy of Holy Week

Dennis Klocek

Copyright © 2025 by Dennis Klocek
All rights reserved

Published 2025
By Soil, Soul and Spirit and Dennis Klocek
Carmichael, California

With support from the Coros Institute at coros.org

Paperback ISBN-13: 979-8-9883689-2-2
eBook ISBN-13: 979-8-9883689-3-9

ACKNOWLEDGMENT

I would like to express my appreciation to those who have made this book possible:

To the original workshop participants in Fair Oaks, CA, April 2015. To Alexis Mei, for his enthusiasm and careful transcription, to Ben Klocek for editorial work, layout and production, to Tanya Coburn for her astute editing, to Daniel Colett and to the donors of Coros Institute for their contributions that made this publication possible.

Dennis Klocek

Contents

ACKNOWLEDGMENT	iii
Foreword by the author	vii
INTRODUCTION	11
OVERVIEW	15
Holy Week Daily Exercise Explanations	21
PALM Sunday – Old and New Sun	25
MONDAY - Cursing the Fig Tree	37
TUESDAY - Judgement and Apocalypse	59
WEDNESDAY - Anointing	81
THURSDAY – Washing of feet	93
FRIDAY – Last Supper and Gethsemane	101
HOLY SATURDAY	121
EASTER SUNDAY	145

Foreword by the author

In the liturgy of Christianity, Holy Week is a key to understanding the Passion of Jesus. In the transformative alchemy of His Passion there is a universal symbolic message for all humans that transcends even Christianity. The message is to work to comprehend the mission of a suffering God.

Many cultures have recognized the intimate emotional linkage between the sufferings of humans and the divine. Many religions have highly valued the willingness of the divine world to suffer along with humans. Dionysos suffered and was brought to life again gestated in the thigh of Zeus. Morally, Osiris was betrayed by another god who was his brother. Osiris suffered but was brought to life again through the magical practice of Isis. Lugh, the shining one, was also betrayed by his brother, Loki the trickster.

In its deepest essence, Holy Week differs from these ancient myths. In the Holy Week drama, the God and the human are the same suffering being. During Holy Week the God/human is betrayed by another human for money. The differing levels of beinghood along with the accompanying guilt, place Holy Week events into human time frames. The drama takes place in the space of a week. That is, it unfolds in time at a human scale. It is not about the drama of gods betraying gods in some far-off time. It is about human beings needing to spiritually transform their time spent on Earth. It is about life today.

The alchemists understood that timing regulates all transformation.

During Holy Week, the timing of each day of the week alchemically, represents a specific action of Christ working among humans to provide new revelations about soul transformation.

Monday, the day of the Moon, is about purifying the astral or moon body. To that end, Christ drives the money changers out of the temple. The warning is about equating business, politics, and religion.

On Tuesday, the day of Mars, Christ wages war against the political and economic burdens inflicted on the common people by the legislative power of the Pharisees, the priests/lawyers of the Hebrews. Again, Christ warns against business/power/politics presented under the guise of religion.

On Wednesday, the day related to Mercury, the god of merchants and thieves, Judas goes to the Pharisees and betrays Christ for money. Apparently, money/power is a fundamental motif in this initial sequence of days.

On Thursday, the day of Jupiter, Christ accepts the task of sacrificing for all humans. In the old pantheon, Jupiter was the ruler or king who was expected to sacrifice his life for his subjects when his time had run out. "The king is dead, long live the king" is an image of this kingly sacrificial deed.

On Friday, the day of Venus, Christ enacts the great sacrament of love for all humanity by giving up his God/human life through suffering at the hands of power elites.

On Saturday, the day of Saturn, Christ descends into hell to purify the ancient and powerfully suffocating forces of evil found in the primal material earth. In the old pantheon, Saturn was seen as a doorway through which karma unfolds. The descent of Christ into the Earth helped the Earth to stay alive. A seed was set for the redemption of human karma that is now available to all humans. That deed of sacrifice forms the basis for the future alchemical transformation of the Earth into a new Sun that will illuminate a new Cosmos.

On Sunday, the day of the Sun, Mary Magdalene meets the risen Christ, thinking that He is a gardener. He is. He has planted a seed in the material earth that will unfold in time.

Holy Week is a time-seed of a future evolution, when humans will find their place among the divine hierarchies. This will be developed by humans recognizing the Cosmic Christ. Christ, the God-human, who dwells in the souls of all beings who suffer. For sure, it will be a long time before that kind of world comes to pass. But it may be that just knowing it can come to pass, can help to lessen the current epidemic of chronic, widespread anxiety about an increasingly uncertain future.

Dennis Klocek
February 2024 Carmichael, California

Alchemy of Holy Week

The following text has been transcribed and edited from a workshop offered in April, 2015 in Fair Oaks, CA.

INTRODUCTION

Welcome everyone. Thanks for coming.

At the last conference we had here on the alchemical laboratory, I was asked something that had been floating around in my mind for a while, which was whether I could do a workshop on the alchemy of Holy Week. A part of me said, "Oh my God, no!" And another part of me said, "You need to do a workshop on the alchemy of Holy Week, man." And so I replied, "Yeah, that sounds like a good idea."

When I got home, I asked myself why I said that, because the issue of Holy Week is not my forte. But as I was preparing for this, I realized I had been studying to do it my whole life. And what I would like to present to you is that the sequence of days in Holy Week is the work in the life of Christian Rosenkreutz. That is why this is the Alchemy of Holy Week.

The Alchemical Wedding of Christian Rosenkreutz starts on Holy Saturday, when he is introduced into the wedding. I just learned that Abraham Lincoln was assassinated on Good Friday, so there are these sorts of pictures in the world of Holy Week as a continually recurring event. It is not something that happened a long time ago. It is an archetype that is unfolding continually, even as we speak. It is an archetypal meditation on the nature of time as the foundation for the new mysteries.

There is a wonderful book by Emil Bock, an anthroposophical scholar, *The Three Years*, where he describes how the passion of

Holy Week is the collision of the old Sun with the new Sun. That theme of the collision of the old mysteries and the new mysteries has its focal point in time in Golgotha. That is the turning point of time, when the old mysteries were dying and the new mysteries were being born. That is the turning point between the clairvoyance that gave rise to fundamentalism, and the clairvoyance that gives rise to freedom. That is the issue in a nutshell and I'm going to keep focusing on that because the whole issue of the Passion and Christ's dialogue, is that he is an insurgent, a deep agitator against the status quo of the Hebrew religion. That is why the priests and the Pharisees persecuted Him. It was political. That is part of what *The Three Years* is about; the political structure of Christ as an insurgent.

But it was not only political. It also had a great deal to do with the nature of clairvoyance and the question of "how do I know that I know?" When an inner picture or imagination of something that I'm working with comes to me, how do I know it is true? This is of the greatest import today because public figures are lying all the time. This will become an accepted fact. And if it becomes just an accepted fact, people will lose contact with what Christ in the gospels called the Son of Man.

We are going to go into what the Son of Man is. Christ is always saying the Son of Man. If you look on the internet for the "Son of Man", you get led to some very strange pictures of what the Son of Man is, as opposed to the Son of God. This is in the language of Holy Week.

Those pictures of the old mystery and the new mystery, and the turning point of the mysteries have to do not only with clairvoyance as a kind of mystery wisdom, but also with the moral issue of clairvoyance, the moral issue of truth telling. It is political.

Christ was not only a religious figure, but also a political figure because of what was going on between the Romans and the Jews at the time in Palestine, and which is still going on today. It is not settled. It is still happening. And that's why it is so important to really understand the issue behind it, behind Holy Week. That is why it involves alchemy and the mission of Christian Rosenkreutz, because the marriage feast is triggered by the ritual death.

These are incredible pictures. In recent years, beheading has been used as political theater. That is why I say that the idea of Holy Week is not only something that happened before; it is happening now. It is of great importance today because of the media and the amplification of imagery having to do with the question of "how do I know that the image I am speaking to you about is true?" That is the difference between the old mysteries and the new mysteries. In the old mysteries, the priests told you what was true. And if you were in line with them, then that was the truth. That is still in the world today. There are whole parts of the world like that; just get in line with what we're telling you, and that's what's true.

Where it gets crazy is when a contemporary person experiences the freedom of their individuality, and they believe that because they are speaking out of an experience that they had, that it is true. We have political figures, with ideas about being presidential candidates, who believe that everything they say is true. Just check the news cycles to get some background on some of the things that are happening today, and you will see Holy Week as a drama of power.

OVERVIEW

Here is a summary of the days in Holy Week.

Palm Sunday/Sun: Old Sun and new Sun in collision.

Monday/Moon: Cursing the fig tree. Old Moon forces of clairvoyance denounced.

Tuesday/Mars: Battle with Pharisees. Retreat to Mount of Olives. Revealing apocalypse to the disciples. Future sheep and goats among humans. Caesar and God.

Wednesday/Mercury: Anointing by Mary Magdalene. Betrayal of Judas. Polarity of Mercury.

Thursday/Jupiter: Washing of the feet. Arrest of Christ. Passover Angel of Death.

Good Friday/Venus: Great deed of love. Sacrifice for others.

Saturday/Saturn: Harrowing of hell.

Easter Sunday: Overcoming of death

We will be working with quotes from the gospels to illustrate these dynamic points about a kind of political/religious drama of the rise of the individual taking power away from the collective. That is what is happening during Holy Week. And the collective is not happy about that – ever.

Easter is what is known as a moveable feast. There have been huge arguments over setting the date of Easter. In fact, the schism in the 600s between the Eastern Church and the Western Church was about setting the dates of Easter. The setting of the date of Easter appears to be random, but it has a very deep significance for the soul life of the human because it is an image of resurrection. Easter happens on the first full Moon after the spring equinox. Why does it happen then?

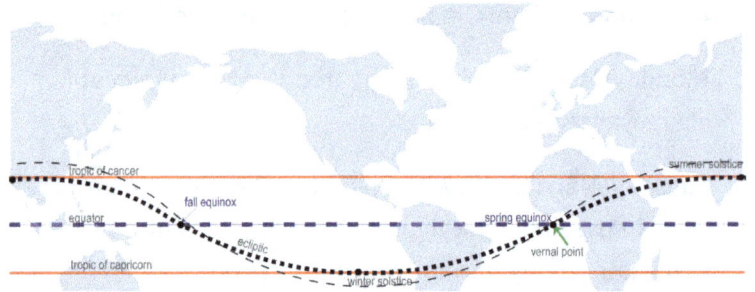

On the diagram, you can see a dotted curved line known as the ecliptic. That is the path of the Sun. The dashed line going through Africa and South America is the equator.

Starting at the left in the map, you can see the dotted line starts at the upper horizontal line. That is the Tropic of Cancer. It then goes to the right and crosses the equator where it says fall equinox. At the fall equinox, the Sun crosses the equator and moves into the southern hemisphere.

It then goes south in declination every day until it reaches the winter solstice at the bottom of the curve due south of Central America.

For those of us in the northern hemisphere, that is our shortest day, when the Sun is in the southern hemisphere. This was very significant in the ancient world because it was understood that when the Sun was at its deepest point in the southern hemisphere, it was actually occulted by the Earth and the forces that were present in the Sun rayed through the Earth as if it were transparent. It was a kind of beginning of a rejuvenation cycle.

When a planet stands in front of another one, there is a kind of damming up of forces that they both share. So the winter solstice was called the dark Sun, the Sun at midnight. It was raying up through the Earth. The druids had all kinds of rituals to be able to perceive this through the Earth. It was a very significant time for them, the beginning of a new cycle, but the new cycle does not give birth until the Sun moves in declination up again, and crosses the equator going north over Western Africa.

When the Sun crosses the equator going north, we get what is called the vernal or spring equinox. Equinox means equal night, where there are 12 hours of day and 12 hours of night, occuring every year around March 20 in the northern hemisphere.

At this time of the year, there are huge amounts of forces available in the natural world to plants and animals which require 12 hours of day and 12 hours of night (12 and 12) for their new cycle to begin. Whole cycles of pest management, budding, and fruiting, and many other things are triggered by the vernal equinox, the spring point of a new year.

In terms of nature, in terms of life forces, in terms of the Earth, the Sun at the equinox was considered to be going through a kind of a birth; the birth of the Sun. This becomes our experience of Eastertide. We celebrate it. But that force of the new Sun is also the beginning of a death process. It is like going into a tunnel; are you going in or are you going out?

So in the ancient times, this beginning was understood to have a kind of virginal quality of potentials which would eventually unfold for three months towards the summer solstice, when a death process would then start to happen. The early spring flowers would reach the summer solstice, set seed, and then start to die away. The annuals are part of this cycle. The annuals, which includes most of the vegetables and grains, are a kind of microcosm of the birth of the Sun at the vernal point. In astrology, the vernal point of your birth chart is the "truth of your life". So that means that when the Sun goes through this spot there is a new possibility, a new Sun. Easter is the new Sun.

Now the Moon, represented on our map diagram by a very faint dashed line, follows the Sun as it goes down below the ecliptic, and then above the ecliptic. The Moon however is eccentric five degrees north and south. It is kind of all over the sky. The Sun then represents the life body, because it is so regular, and the Moon, the astral body, because it is kind of all over the place.

Now there are certain instances where the ether force of the Sun and the astral force of the Moon come together in a very intense space, resulting in what is called an eclipse, and the place where this happens is on the ecliptic.

So the relationship between the Sun and the Moon and the Earth is huge, especially regarding the way in which the life forces of the human, and the soul forces of the human interact in consciousness. This is clairvoyance. Clairvoyance comes either from the ego/astral side or from the astral/etheric side.

We have talked about this for years: how is your clairvoyance arising? That is a drama of the Sun and the Moon. For that, I would like to read a quote from Rudolf Steiner. This is from page 60 of *Christ And The Spiritual World*:

"The working together of thinking, feeling and willing has to be kept in order. Not, however, from all the planets, but only through the Sun, the Moon and the Earth. So that through the interworking of the Sun, the Moon and the Earth, if this is harmonious, the human being is made fit for the harmonious cooperation of their three soul powers."

Rudolf Steiner calls this the Virgin Moon at Easter. It is the first full Moon after the Sun crosses the equator. The Sun is virginal and the Moon follows it, and also has its virginal qualities. The first full Moon, followed by the following dark Moon after the equinox, are equal in power in terms of plant growth, and that is what gives a surge to the annuals.

The Moon gets its virginity again, so to speak, and that enables plants to have a superfluity of life forces that allow them to surge up off the Earth in their annual growth spurt. It is really quite remarkable how the first full Moon followed by the dark Moon after the equinox (after the Sun goes through the vernal point) are equal in their power. Since the dark Moon following Easter is the Virgin Moon and is equivalent to the full Moon preceding it, there is so much procreative power for new potential. The procreative power for the new mysteries, the new potential. It is what is happening in nature. It is what is happening within the planetary spheres. It is what is happening in the soul of the human. It is the possibility of assimilating the shadow element to the degree that it can become a medicine. This is the alchemical wedding.

The way we are going to work with the idea of this new mystery alchemically is that each day there is a glyph that can be used as a meditative device to help you enter into the dynamics of Holy Week. The glyph will be given at the end of each chapter for the following day. The idea is to work with the glyph in the evening and let it spend time in our consiousness overnight.

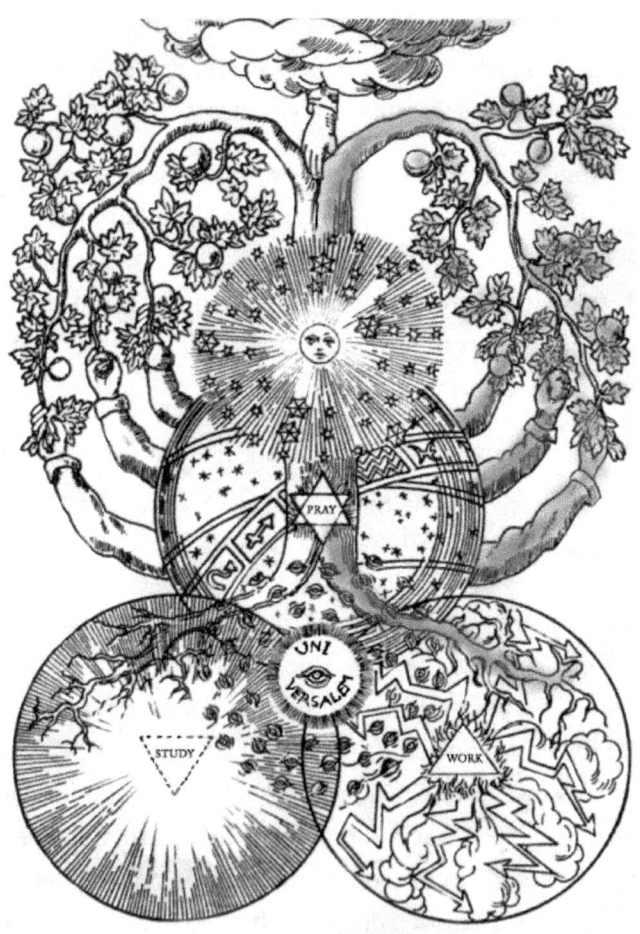

Holy Week Daily Exercise Explanations
The Glyph and the Crucible

In order to journey deeper, each day you will be given the opportunity to take a corresponding glyph into sleep. Then in the morning, we are going to do an exercise called "the crucible".

We will do the crucible exercise every morning and will take a glyph into sleep the night before as it relates to the Tree of Knowledge drawing (see figure above). During the crucible exercise with your partner, you are only allowed to ask questions. You are not allowed to make a comment. For a contemporary soul, that is like a crucible. Opinion is the enemy.

This way of ordering is a microcosm of the way the Rosicrucians worked by taking a glyph into sleep and then in the morning asking questions with no answers.

Christ talked to the apostles on Holy Tuesday about the Apocalypse. He said, "This is going to be really weird for you people, I want you to just meditate and pray, but don't come up with answers beforehand. If you expect answers beforehand, I can't help you."

So keeping the question open is the crucible that we have to learn to live with in order to live a creative life when life looks like ninety yards of barbed wire for breakfast. What happens then is that we go into blame and opinion and guilt and shame. The new mysteries are about keeping the question open long enough until you can be led, because if you come up with the answers ahead of time, Christ cannot help you. Just do the work in freedom and keep the question open. That's the new clairvoyance. Don't say anything is true until you hear it from someone else. Only then can you know that you haven't manipulated things with your opinion.

Working with the Glyphs

Let's look at this row of glyphs.

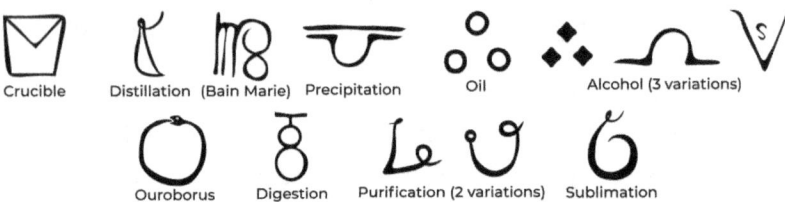

The first glyph on the left, which looks like an envelope, is the one for a crucible. The square is Earth. The square means "you are here". The triangle pointing down is also Earth, or Earth in earth. In the crucible, we burn things until they become complete earth. They are no longer living. They become what an alchemist would call a corpse. As we will find out, the resurrection of the corpse is the central mystery of Holy Week. It is also the central mystery of alchemy because it is a language of the way in which a corpse has been formed from the old mysteries and must be put into a crucible and annihilated so that the new mysteries can arise out of it.

There is a glyph for each day. You can find these glyphs in an alchemical formula.

After the glyph on the left for crucible, then there is distillation, precipitation, oil and alcohol, ouroboros, digestion, purification, sublimation. These are the glyphs representing the processes for all the days of Holy Week.

> Crucible – Sunday
>
> Distillation (Bain Marie) – Monday
>
> Precipitation – Tuesday
>
> Oil and Alcohol – Wednesday
>
> Ouroboros – Thursday
>
> Digestion – Friday
>
> Purification – Saturday
>
> Sublimation – Sunday

Every evening: Inwardly drawing a glyph, then taking it into sleep.

Every morning: Drawing the glyph inwardly, then working in "the crucible" by asking questions about how the glyph relates to the Tree of Knowledge image.

Why do we use a glyph like this? Because if you think it in words, you get stuck, your imagination can't grasp it. The alchemists used a glyph meditatively to tune their personal feelings into universal, archetypal feelings of the world soul, feelings that the Earth is having in relation to the Sun and the Moon, to the life body and the astral body.

You can meditate on each day of Holy Week by inwardly drawing and erasing the glyph of the process that is connected to that day. When you make a glyph and are drawing it inwardly, you are placing your consciousness into the field of geometry of those movements. The glyph is not the finished thing, but the process that you use to draw it, the movement of the glyph, is the healing. What you're meditating on in the glyph is the process of going from manifestation to its spiritual condition.

Taking a glyph into sleep: Before you go to sleep, draw the form of the glyph in your imagination. Keep working on it so that you have the experience that you and the glyph begin to shake hands. At a certain point, it becomes very easy for you to visualize making it. You can hold it and build it and move it. You can get to the point where it is doing it. That's the shaking hands.

If you really want to engage with this, inwardly draw the symbol and then erase it in the opposite order of how you drew it. When you do that, your consciousness participates in the movement of the symbol by lifting it away from its corpus. You're entering into its dynamic. Then allow the image to dissolve into silence and emptiness in your imagination, then go to sleep.

On each day of Holy Week you can meditate on the day by forming and inwardly dissolving the glyph of the process connected to that day.

Glyph for Palm Sunday

Crucible

In Holy Week, Christ is coming from Galilee, a kind of a rural district, into Jerusalem and He knows that his arrival will stir the pot.

PALM Sunday – Old and New Sun

Matthew 21:2-9 As they approached Jerusalem and came to Bethphage on the Mount of Olives, Jesus sent two disciples, saying to them, "Go to the village ahead of you, and at once you will find a donkey tied there, with her colt by her. Untie them and bring them to me. If anyone says anything to you, say that the Lord needs them, and he will send them right away." This took place to fulfill what was spoken through the prophet: "Say to Daughter Zion, 'See, your king comes to you, gentle and riding on a donkey, and on a colt, the foal of a donkey'." The disciples went and did as Jesus had instructed them. They brought the donkey and the colt and placed their cloaks on them for Jesus to sit on. A very large crowd spread their cloaks on the road, while others cut branches from the trees and spread them on the road. The crowds that went ahead of him and those that followed shouted, "Hosanna to the Son of David!"

Jesus at the Temple

Matthew 21:12-13 Jesus entered the temple courts and drove out all who were buying and selling there. He overturned the tables of the money changers and the benches of those selling doves. "It is written," he said to them, "'My house will be called a house of prayer,' but you are making it 'a den of robbers.'"

Palm Sunday is the entry into what could be called the crucible of Holy Week.

A crucible is a place where you lead substances into a crucifixion. Alchemically, the crucible involves taking substances and burning them.

On Palm Sunday, Christ was entering the crucible. He was entering Jerusalem, where it was all going to happen. He was going into the crucible. The new mysteries are about feelings, but not personal feelings. Rather, they are about feeling extracts; the feelings of the world soul. The feelings of the world soul are the movements of the planets – how the Earth is interacting with the Sun and the Moon, for example. Those relationships, angular aspects, approaches, avoidances and occultations are feelings having to do with deep Pythagorean geometries. These are the feelings of the world soul.

When you make a glyph and draw it as an inner picture, what is happening inwardly is that you are placing your consciousness into the field of the geometry of those movements, like a loop or a square which has tension. The alchemist used a glyph meditatively to tune their personal feelings into the universal, archetypal feelings of the world soul.

The drama of Christ during Holy Week – Monday: Moon day,

Tuesday: Mars day, Wednesday: Woden or Mercury day – is to travel through the planets and their mood qualities to redeem them on Easter Sunday, the new Sun.

This is a symbolic language that the alchemist used to come in contact with certain feelings. Not personal feelings, but rather feelings that the Earth is having in relation to the Sun and the Moon, to the life body and the astral body.

So why do we use a glyph like this? Because if you think it in words, you get stuck. Your imagination can't grasp it. And your imagination is the thing that is at risk with fundamentalism.

Fundamentalism is to take your imagination and put it in abeyance somewhere, so that you can believe what they believe. They don't want you to imagine something else. They want you to get in line with what they believe. Pharisee law #231: "Before you can drink from the cup, you must wash the outside of the cup with running water." We will have a look at a quote for Tuesday of Holy Week where Christ talks about the irony of washing the outside of the cup. "Oh, you wash the outside of the cup? Why don't you wash your soul? Why don't you do what you do to the cup to yourself? Then the Son of Man could come and speak to you."

Let's start off with our first crucible exercise. On the Tree of Knowledge image, look at the picture of the hand coming out of the cloud. It's touching a tree, and the tree is split. One side of the tree is light. One side is dark. And there is fruit on the tree. The cloud, the hand, and the split tree are the subject of our crucible exercise. Don't go down to the hands reaching up. That is another level. For five minutes, look at this part of the image and if a question comes to you, ask your partner (or write it in your journal if doing this exercise alone). State the question as a complete sentence. Then wait a bit and live with it to see how it feels before asking the next question. You are now burning the corpus in the crucible of your own belief. The goal of this exercise is to watch the movement in your own soul coming from someone else's question. By asking questions that don't get answered, we are creating a field of consciousness. The crucible is the feeling in your soul that comes from another person's question. So that if you think someone's question is coming from left field, then you just learn how to play the outfield. That is very healthy if you can tolerate it. If there is something in the question that you cannot answer, that is a kind of burning that an alchemist would use to reduce it down to its essence and you're doing that by asking questions that don't get answered.

This is one of the big messages of Holy Week. "Can you tolerate people not going along with your program?" The Jews are being put down by the Romans and the common people are being put down by the Pharisees. This is the political structure that Christ is speaking into because there were dire consequences in the ancient mysteries around power. "I have power over you because I have the clairvoyance to see your faults when I can see your faults according to my checklist." This goes far beyond Holy Week, it is the basis of the Inquisition in the 1600s, and of Nazism. It is not lost from our world today.

At the time of Christ, the Romans were taking over everything. The Jewish people were trying to find their place. It wasn't until 1948 that they established Israel and it's been an issue ever since. There was all of this opinion and conflict around the issue of "you need to get in line with what I believe". That was the thrust of the drama of Holy Week.

I. Palm Sunday

This is Palm Sunday. This is in Matthew 21.

"As they approached Jerusalem and came to Bethphage on the Mount of Olives, Jesus sent two disciples ahead, saying to them, "Go into the village ahead of you and immediately you will find a donkey tied and a colt with her. Untie them and bring them to me. If anyone says anything to you just say this, 'The Lord needs them. And he will send them immediately.' This took place to fulfill what had been spoken through the prophet."

This prophecy is clairvoyance. During the time of Christ, if you were a holy person, you were expected to do miracles. You were expected to be able to prophesy. You were expected to be able to see into another person. The training that you would receive, especially in the temple sleep process, trained you to get access to that dimension and hold it in your life body in a particular configuration. You were taught to do that. You were not considered a holy person unless you could prophesy and heal the sick.

Steiner himself said that people being brought back from the dead had been done before but it was never done by a soul who had never incarnated before. This is where we get to the depth of the mystery of the phantom.

For an idea of someone coming back from the dead, look at the issue in China about the Dalai Lama where the Chinese are politicizing the reincarnation of the new Dalai Lama. They want to be the ones to pick the new Dalai Lama to make sure that he is in line with their political structure. They want to be part of the decision.

But the Dalai Lama responded by saying, "I am not reincarnating. So anyone you choose is bogus." Why? In order to keep sacred what is sacred. This is in the news. If the Chinese pick the new Dalai Lama, is there a real Dalai Lama? It is bogus because he said he is not coming back. These are the new mysteries.

He will come back but not as a Dalai Lama. And therefore without the powers that he had. Rudolf Steiner talked about spiritual leaders reincarnating but without the powers that they had accrued in a previous incarnation. This is also a part of the new mysteries.

If you read the Alchemical Wedding, when Christian Rosenkreutz takes the oath of the knight of the golden stone on the seventh day, that is about not having powers that you had before and not extending your life beyond its normal time. He had to take a vow not to do that.

And to continue with Matthew 21:

Tell the daughter of Zion, "See your king that is coming to you gentle and riding on a donkey and on a colt the foal of a donkey." The disciples went and did as Jesus had instructed them. They brought the donkey and the colt and placed their cloaks for Jesus to sit on. A very large crowd spread the cloaks on the road, while others cut branches from the trees and spread them on the road. The crowds that went ahead of him, and those that followed, shouted "Hosanna to the Son of David."

The Son of David is the one who was going to lift up the Jews from their subjugation by the Romans and set the stage for Jerusalem to become what was prophesied. So he was the Son of David, the Son of God, the Son of Man.

Why a donkey? Everything in the gospels is symbolic of a level of consciousness. The Son of Man is symbolic of a level of consciousness. The donkey is symbolic of a level of consciousness. I will give you some examples of donkeys as symbols through the ages.

In the myth of King Midas, Midas was a devotee of Dionysos. As the myth goes, Midas was approached by Apollo with his lyre, who asked Midas if he would like to be a devotee of Apollo. Midas said no because he was a devotee of Dionysos who basically sings the songs of the common man. Then Midas said, "Let's have a contest." So Apollo and Dionysos both played, and they asked Midas which one he preferred. Midas said he preferred Dionysos and then went to sleep. And in the morning he woke up with the ears of a donkey. He grew the ears of an ass to listen to the songs of Dionysos. After that, he always wore a funny hat that he could fold his ears into. But every once in a while, he had to go down the river to wash his face and take his hat off. And the reeds saw his ears and they whispered in the wind to each other, "Midas has the ears of an ass."

What does that wonderful myth suggest? That the clairvoyance of Dionysos is the old blood clairvoyance. It is ancient. My body is telling me what's going on.

Another example is "The Golden Ass" by Apuleius. It is the story of the journey of a young man, trying to deal with his rather interesting sexual appetites. He goes to a witches coven, has all sorts of interesting adventures, and he also turns into an ass.

Then there is the fairy tale of "The Prince and the Donkey". The donkey is the old clairvoyance, and it takes love, compassion and understanding from a princess to help him drop the donkey suit and become a prince once again. Old clairvoyance; new clairvoyance.

There is also Shakespeare's "A Midsummer Night's Dream," where Bottom gets the ears of an ass and turns into a donkey. Why does he turn into a donkey? Because it is a tale of the old clairvoyance.

So Christ comes into Jerusalem on a donkey. And the people say the liberator has come who is going to lift us from this subjugation. The Son of David has finally come to us.

By this time, Christ had been performing miracles and healings with crowds of people following him in the wilderness. Stories were spreading throughout the countryside that he was the great prophet whose power would finally shake off Roman rule and establish the new kingdom, the new Jerusalem on Earth, that everyone was expecting.

So He rides into Jerusalem on a donkey. This is instinctual wisdom, what Rufolf Steiner called "belly clairvoyance". And He was sitting on it, so that the people would know that this is the end for this old clairvoyance.

After that triumphant entrance on the donkey, the first thing that He does is to go to the temple where there is buying and selling. This is from Matthew 21:12:

Jesus entered the temple courts and drove out those who were buying and selling there. He overturned the benches and tables of the money changers and those who were selling doves.

That was not an acceptable thing to do because these were turtle doves. The people bought them to give to the priests as payment. So if you wanted to come and tithe, there were sellers of turtle doves that you could buy to give to the priests. It was a tax service basically, but it was a religious tax service.

"It is written," he said to them, "'My house will be called a house of prayer but you are making it a den of robbers."

So He comes riding on the old clairvoyance and He says, "I hear you calling me the Son of David, but I know that at the end of the week there is going to be a whole other regime happening here." Christ knew that. And He went into the temple and said the new mysteries are not about selling doves. There is something else that needs to happen in this house.

When He said to the money changers and the sellers of tribute money that they had to get out of the temple, that was not acceptable to the regime because that was the way things were done.

Emil Bock gives a wonderful picture of that. Christ came from Galilee, which was equivalent today to coming from some place like Tahoe and going to San Francisco. He came from this bucolic location and went into Jerusalem where all the wheeling and dealing was done by the powers that be who ran the temple.

Here, the common people were subjugated not only by the Romans but also by the priests and the Pharisees. So there was a whole system to the way things happened and whether or not it was allowed for you to wash your clothes on Saturday, or whatever the rule was.

Many of the parables that Christ gave have that flavor to them, the gist being that the coin of the realm in the spiritual world is prayer and attention to the divine. By using simple parables that seemed to be about usury or tithing, He was really talking about a higher level that He called the Son of Man.

All through the gospels, Christ is using this language of the Son of Man. The Son of Man is what in today's esoteric language we would call the Virgin Sophia. The Virgin Sophia is the soul purified of desire. Each individual soul helps constitute that Sophianic consciousness by contributing an organ of perception.

We are building in Sophianic consciousness, the new Jerusalem, an organ of perception of the Holy Spirit. Those organs of perception are what Rudolf Steiner called Manas, Buddhi, Atman. They are the transformed physical body, transformed life body and transformed soul. Taken together, they form a spiritual body that will be us at the end of time, that is, the Son of Man.

When Christ is speaking here, He is speaking to the apostles or the people about the end times when the Son of Man will be recognized. The Son of God is your body that you inherit from Adam and Eve. And you have to give it back. The Son of Man is your manhood and womanhood to overcome the corpse.

The corpse is the residue of the unperceived desires that makes in your soul a shadow body, a dense body, a corpus, alchemically, an ash.

So the Son of Man is the Christ force in each soul working to make us aware of how to transform desire into wish, resolve and love. It is the same force, it is just purified. In alchemy, that is what you do in the crucible; you purify things by burning them into a corpse.

Glyph for Monday – Distillation

Now I am going to draw on the board the glyph for distillation. It is the second in the row of glyphs. The glyph is not the finished thing, but in the process that you use to draw it, in the movement of the glyph, is the healing.

I. Palm Sunday

Distillation (Bain Marie)

The first glyph is a standard distillation.

The second glyph is another kind of distillation known as Mary's bath, the 'bain Marie'. It is a very slow distillation in water. Put the water in a retort, heat the water and there is an ascending and descending of the vapors in the retort. Then it goes through an inversion from manifestation into a spiritual form. So distillation is lifting the corpus into a spiritual condition.

Taking a glyph into sleep: Before you go to sleep, draw the form of the glyph. Keep working on it so that you have the experience that you and the glyph begin to shake hands. At a certain point, it becomes very easy for you to visualize making it. You hold it and build it and move it. You get to the point where it is just doing it. That's shaking hands. Do that before you go to sleep. What you're meditating on in the glyph is the process of going from manifestation to its spiritual condition.

This type of meditation would be given in the old days as a kind of preparation. You would visualize the symbols. There was music written about these kinds of processes, chord sequences, and all this literature around glyphs. The essence of the alchemical work is to work inwardly with symbols to reach the archetypal beings that stand behind them.

You can choose to work on whichever one seems to speak to

you. The first one starts at the base and goes directly up into nothingness; I cook it and it goes up. The other is where you put your retort and a big container of water and heat it gently and there's a circulation and the vapour goes up, hits the side wall and comes down. It's a circulating gesture. Choose whichever appeals to you.

Refer to the crucible drawing, the Tree of Knowledge image. We will have five minutes of crucible work, which means only asking questions. Look at the picture, focusing on the section with three arms with hands reaching out on the left, and then the three arms and hands on the right. The questions should be about that section. As we go along, you will see how this works.

MONDAY - Cursing the Fig Tree

Matthew 21:18-22 Early in the morning, as Jesus was on his way back to the city, He was hungry. Seeing a fig tree by the road, he went up to it but found nothing on it except leaves. Then He said to it, "May you never bear fruit again!" Immediately the tree withered. When the disciples saw this, they were amazed. "How did the fig tree wither so quickly?" they asked. Jesus replied, "Truly I tell you, if you have faith and do not doubt, not only can you do what was done to the fig tree, but also you can say to this mountain, 'Go, throw yourself into the sea,' and it will be done. If you believe, you will receive whatever you ask for in prayer."

Matthew 22:1-14 The Parable of the Wedding Banquet

Jesus spoke to them again in parables, saying: "The kingdom of heaven is like a king who prepared a wedding banquet for his son. He sent his servants to those who had been invited to the banquet to tell them to come, but they refused to come. Then he sent some more servants and said, 'Tell those who have been invited that I have prepared my dinner: My oxen and fattened cattle have been butchered, and everything is ready. Come to the wedding banquet.'

"But they paid no attention and went off—one to his field, another to his business. The rest seized his servants, mistreated them and killed them. The king was enraged. He sent his army and destroyed those murderers and burned their city.

"Then he said to his servants, 'The wedding banquet is ready, but those I invited did not deserve to come. So go to the street corners and invite to the banquet anyone you find.' So the servants went out into the streets

and gathered all the people they could find, the bad as well as the good, and the wedding hall was filled with guests.

"But when the king came in to see the guests, he noticed a man there who was not wearing wedding clothes. He asked, 'How did you get in here without wedding clothes, friend?' The man was speechless.

"Then the king told the attendants, 'Tie him hand and foot, and throw him outside, into the darkness, where there will be weeping and gnashing of teeth.' For many are invited, but few are chosen."

This morning in the first session, we will focus on Monday of Holy Week, where there is the cursing of the fig tree.

This is a big ticket item, the cursing of the fig tree. Everything in these vignettes is a symbol for the development of the Son of Man. This is Rosicrucian work, the work of self transformation: to transform one's soul into a higher being, the Sophia. In ancient times, that work was given to the people by the priesthood. It was given out of a tradition of "this is how it should be done".

As Steiner spoke about it, the seven holy Rishis were so embedded in the spiritual world that they had a direct experience of the difference between the Adamic body, the body of flesh, and the spiritual body. Because of their direct experience, they said, "Do not go down into the Adamic body because it is just maya." But as time evolved, it was necessary for humans to engage with the earth. In Persia this was through Zarathustra, who taught humanity to plow the earth to let the light in. Then we had the great god of light, Ahura Mazda and the great god of darkness, Ahriman, teaching of the splitting away from the spiritual world into the struggle with the shadow. By the time you get to Egypt, there is the cult of death. Then in Greece, "better a beggar on Earth than a king in the realm of the shades". Steiner talks about this whole process of consciousness coming down.

By the time of Golgotha, human consciousness on Earth had become so fixed that everything about the inner life was promulgated by the authorities and if you did not accept it, you were exiled.

This is Roman law, and today we are in its last gasp. Here it's called "Republicans and Democrats". No one can get along because there are so many laws that everything becomes lawless. Lawlessness rules because as soon as you walk out your door, you risk becoming a perpetrator. Get in your car and drive down the road? There is a speed limit for that. This is Roman rule, where everything is promulgated from the outside. But everyone who is in that rule of law is pushing the envelope and saying, "I don't think so."

This struggle is the reason Christ had to come back.

So, why a fig tree? The fig tree in its reproductive cycle has a unique flowering process which involves something called a caprifig. When the fig flowers, the caprifig comes out first, but it is infertile and falls off. People often freak out when their fig tree loses all its early figs. It has this kind of first fake flowering which falls off, and then the reproductive flower comes out. This second flowering is very unusual because the anthers and stamens of the reproductive organs of the fig are inside the fruit. There is a little hole in the bottom of the fig. Very often when you get a fig you will see a little drop of nectar there. That is because that hole was opened and inside the fig were the flowers of the fig.

Little wasps about the size of a pinhead can enter through that hole. They are fig wasps. The females go in and create a boudoir inside the fig. They send out a pheromone, and the males come. If you watch, you can see the males hovering around that opening. They enter it and have a little bacchanalia in there that fertilizes the fig from the inside. The picture is that all of the real power is hidden on the inside. This is the iconostasis of the Eastern church; you are not allowed to see where the power is except when the priesthood determines that it is time, and then the priest opens the door and you are allowed to see it, until the door closes again.

A few years ago, I went on a pilgrimage to Czestochowa in Poland to see the Madonna. There was a door on the Madonna. All of the faithful were down in the cathedral. A trumpet sounded, and the door opened and a little later, a trumpet sounded again and the door closed. That gesture – something is hidden from you until a certain time when you are allowed to see it before it is hidden again – is a sign of the old clairvoyance, the old mysteries that Christ is seeking to overcome.

What you will see in the old clairvoyance is determined by the tradition you are trained in. In order to be clairvoyant, you have to go to a school of the priesthood, where they will tell you that when you are in this consciousness, you will see this being who will speak to you and tell you something. And when you come back, the priests will ask, "Did this being tell you this or not?" If it told you something else, then you failed the test. That was the way it was. That is the old clairvoyance. The fig tree and the way in which it holds its fruit so that its reproductive cycle is hidden is an example of the old clairvoyance.

With that picture in mind, if you read the gospel story again, it says that Jesus was hungry and He saw the fig but He found nothing but leaves.

II. Monday

Now look at the Tree of Knowledge image again. Look at the hands. One or two of them are finding nothing but leaves. Only one of them is getting the real deal.

Then He said to the fig tree, "May you never bear fruit again!" He is saying that the old clairvoyance, the old mysteries, the old way in which you were asked to participate in the mysteries is done and will never bear fruit again.

The tree withered, and the disciples asked how He did that.

He answered, "If you have faith and do not doubt, you can do this and more. You can tell the mountain, that is the law, the rule, the organization, to go take a hike."

If you do not doubt, if you have faith, you can do this. Faith in what? In the system? No. In prayer. We have to learn how to pray. If you believe, you will receive whatever you ask for in prayer. He says that again and again and again. Because it is in the prayer life that you come in contact with the Son of Man.

In the parable of the cursing of the fig tree, He is speaking about how the new mysteries will be enacted. It will require a lot of work on the part of the person.

Then in Matthew 22, we have the parable of the wedding banquet. *And Jesus spoke to them again in parables. The kingdom of heaven is like a king preparing a wedding banquet for his son.* This is about Christ as the bridegroom. This is not about the king preparing his own wedding banquet. It is about the King, the Father God, preparing a wedding for His Son.

Christ is describing Himself – and us. This is the alchemical wedding. That is the setting. So the King, the Father God, sends his servants to those who had been invited. In the past, that was the chosen elite, the priesthood, the ones who held the keys to the mysteries.

So the servants, that is, the hierarchies, the Angels and Archangels, were sent to the chosen elite to invite them to the wedding where there was going to be a new bridegroom and a new way of doing things. Aren't you excited? But they refused to come.

And he sent more servants to tell those who had been invited to come to the wedding banquet. "Everything is prepared. My fattened oxen and cattle have been butchered and everything is ready. Come to the wedding banquet! Show up for the new bridegroom and the new way of doing things. Come on down – it will be great!" But they paid no attention. One went to his field and another to his business.

So He is setting the stage here. He is saying that the ones He has chosen are just making a business out of this. They do not want to come to the banquet.

Finally, those he invited seized His servants and mistreated and killed them.

Then the King was enraged and sent his army to destroy these murderers and their city. The King said, *"Those whom I invited did not deserve to come."* They have betrayed the mysteries.

I have read several books on the history of the mysteries, and the scholars agree that what destroyed the old mysteries was power and sorcery. Power wars and sorcery wars over occult power. Today that war is in the realm of devices. It has moved from "I'll do power over you with my mind" to "I'll do power over you with

II. Monday

my nuclear armaments", for example.

So those who were invited did not come. Then the King said to his servants, "Go into the streets and invite to the banquet anyone you can find." This is the new mystery: it is you and me. Good and bad. "Go into the streets and gather all of the people, the bad as well as the good." And then the wedding hall was filled with guests.

But when the King came in to see the guests, he noticed a man who was not wearing wedding clothes. In the mysteries, this refers to the difference between what is known as the garment and the body. Only those with a spotless garment can enter, as it says in the Bible. Your garment is who you will be at the end times. Your body is the Adamic body that you are given and you take on and off as a vehicle for doing the work.

You cannot do this work unless you are in a body of flesh. That is also part of the new mysteries. You have to have a physical body in order to build a spiritual body because your experience in a body of flesh is what you contribute to the new Jerusalem. No one else can have that because you are the only one in the body of flesh that you are issued for that particular incarnation. This is the basis of the new mysteries.

How you experience your incarnation is the key; the vehicle for building the new body of Manas, Buddhi and Atman to make the Virgin Sophia. That is part of the new mysteries.

This guest who shows up in his Adamic body but hasn't put on his wedding garment; he is not doing the work. He was invited to the wedding, and he thought he could come in street clothes and it would be taken care of.

And he was asked, "How did you get in here without wedding clothes?" This means, "Why are you not doing the work here?" The bridegroom is about to come in. And the King told the attendants to tie him up, hand and foot, and throw him out into the darkness. He is living in the darkness because he hasn't taken up the work. *And there will be weeping and gnashing of teeth. For many are invited but few are chosen.*

In the new mysteries, everyone is invited. The priests no longer turn up when you are two years old to take you away and train you. You already have an invitation. It is called your belly button. You are in the club. And that is your invitation to the wedding feast of the bridegroom and the bride.

Who is the bride? It is your soul. And Christ is the bridegroom. And when you are invited to the wedding, you have to drop your street clothes and dress with style.

When read that way, this is not about a wedding. It is about the future. The bible passages we'll be reading are about the method of the new mysteries. The purpose of the New Testament is to make it clear that the old mysteries where you were told what to do from the outside are done. Those days are done.

That is why Christ had to come back and go through the Passion. It was to show the way it has to be done in the new mysteries. "Do this in remembrance of me." Here is what is going to happen if you take this up. This is Holy Week.

And there is a fundamental issue behind this. Alchemically, to achieve this, you have to do something to go against what was known as "fiat".

Refer to the following alchemical diagram by Robert Fludd, an alchemist. It is a picture of the drama of the fall into bodies that were made of matter and were sense perceptible. It depicts the original creation or the creation of the Father God. There is a cloud with a hand coming out of it. Written in the cloud is the word "fiat". Fiat means "I create". The hand of God coming from the fiat cloud is creating the creation, the original creation. The original creation creates the Adamic body in alchemy. The Adamic body had an original form in the creation, but fiat creates a problem for the Father. All you have to do is raise teenagers and you understand it. You create and they take your car to go to a beer party in Tijuana. You can't control them.

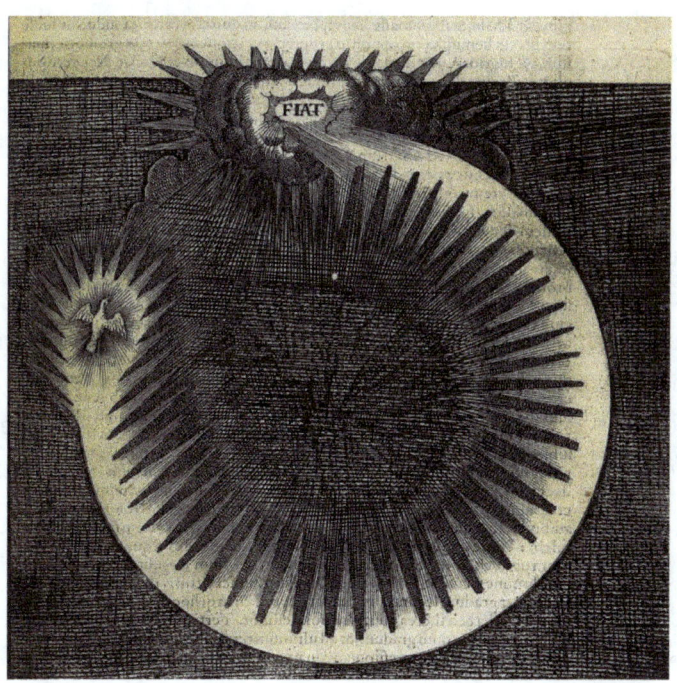

So the fiat creates the creation, which is no longer the creator. It is "a creation". And the creation is one step removed from the creator. It is on its way to becoming something other than the original intent of the creator. This is the problem of the fall, the fall of humanity, back in the day.

And the agent that carried that was the Holy Spirit. Here we see the Holy Spirit being sent by the Creator to go out in time and return to this circle. The diagram shows the wing beats of the Holy Spirit going out through time and coming back to create the form of a circle. The circle is the Christ coming from the original creation of the Father God, created through fiat that goes out and comes back again, reformed. In between there are all these wing beats; all of these epochs of time in which humans will be recalled, late and slow, through the action of the Holy Spirit. In the void in the center is the realm of the Christ being that has to come from being one with the Father to being trashed by ignorant human beings. Then saying, "That's OK, you can't really kill me."

You can read the precedent for that in the dialogue in the *Bhagavad Gita* between Krishna and Arjuna on the battlefield. Krishna tells Arjuna over and over, "Do you think you're going to kill all these people? You're not going to kill all these people, you're only going to kill their bodies." You can't kill them because why? Because you didn't make them. You don't have the power to kill them because you're not big enough. That's way before Holy Week.

So this is a theme, the difference between the Adamic physical body and the spiritual body. The Son of Man, as Christ keeps referring to it, is a new spiritual body made by the will of each individual to live a better life. As we do that, it has to be done in freedom, or it would just be part of the original creation.

II. Monday

The problem with the original creation is that it is like clockwork; this happens and then that happens. This one begat that one and that one begat this one. That is the Old Testament. Do this and this is what happens to you if you do it. Today that kind of consciousness leads to fundamentalism. It doesn't matter what religion it is. It could be economics. Fundamentalism is a problem because it denies the freedom that Christ died for.

Whether you are a fundamentalist economist or you were raised in a repressive religious atmosphere, you are still a fundamentalist. If you're an atheist, you are saying, "Everyone else is really stupid except for me and those who believe in the same thing." The gesture of fundamentalism is that I and my buddies are right and everyone else is wrong. Whether it's ISIS or ISIL or the Jesuits or any sectarian aspect of a religion or a political movement. Hitler rose to power on what could be called a green party platform. It was one soil. The Earth mother was Germany. The father was the Führer. And when there was a marriage, they would have a superhuman. This is fundamentalism.

The fundamentalist gesture is "I'm in a club that no-one else is in". There's even fundamentalist anthroposophy: "my way or the highway". That gesture of the fundamental, of restriction of *your* belief, that "*your* belief is stupid" is why Holy Week had to happen.

It has nothing to do with church. The Christ being in Steiner's work is a cosmic being. He is not Jesus. Jesus had a whole other mission. Although it is difficult to understand how that happened, you can read about the two Jesus children in Steiner's work. It explains, in an esoteric alchemical language how it was possible to create a vehicle that could stand having what is known as "the human phantom" as part of its structure. I'm trying to build a case for the human phantom which is what Christian Rosenkreutz came back to teach about. We will get there as we go along. The human phantom was the unique part of the cosmic Christ being, that Christ brought into a body of flesh – and that changed a lot of possibilities which I will explain as we go along.

For years, I asked many people, "What is the human phantom?" Nobody would really answer me until I found it myself in Steiner's texts. I could tell you but it doesn't really make much sense until you "get it". When you get what the human phantom is, the deed of Christ makes a lot of sense. Until then, it's just another fundamentalist belief.

In order to understand that, we have to understand a bit of alchemical practice.

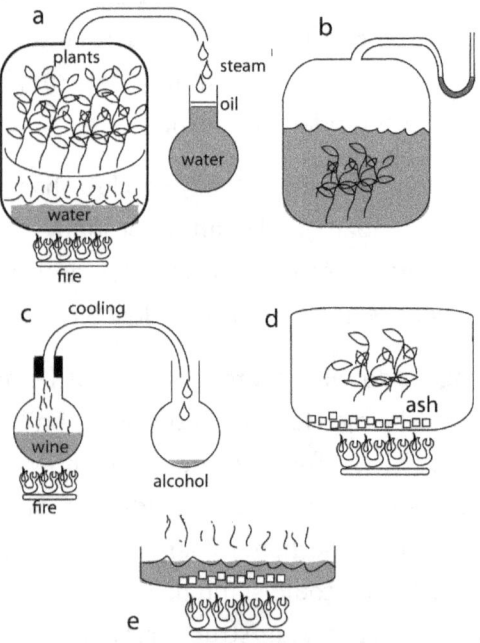

Look at figure *a, b, c, d, e* which describes something called a spagyric process. It means "to take apart and put back together again". It comes from the work of Paracelsus, the great alchemist.

It is understood in alchemy that the substances of the original creation, the Adamic body, the body of flesh, the body of substance, includes the forces of attraction within substances – molecular forces we would call them today – and the actual substance itself. The forces of the substances, their attraction and repulsion, are not the actual substance itself. You can take calcium and put it on a shelf and it will sit there until the end of time. All you need to do is put it into a weak acid solution and it becomes interactive.

It is in the space between things where there are forces. Where the forces stop, the substances appears. That is a fundamental alchemical law. Where a process stops, a substance appears.

And when the substance comes in contact with another substance that it has an affinity for – in chemistry it is called an elective affinity like a base has a relationship to an acid – something happens. When those two substances come in contact, forces that are engendered that are not part of the substance itself but part of a field that the two substances have entered.

The field is the spiritual dimension of the becoming of the substance. This is a new kind of chemistry. If you can find a chemist who is not a fundamentalist, they become interested in this because they recognize that what they are working with is something that is intangible; it's mathematical. How many moles of this and how many moles of that and they get a titration where you get a salt. Those are words that they use but they see things happen that are invisible. They have all kinds of theories about it. Every time there is a discovery, they have to change the rules again. I have talked to many chemists about this, because it's a convention.

We live in a funny world where we think there's a reality but most of science is convention. Astronomy – convention. Chemistry – convention. Biology – convention. Convention helps us to not to freak out because we don't know anything. If we realized what we didn't know, it would be really bad.

The alchemists understood that the original creation had what they call "feces" in their language – dead waste, shadow in it. The substance was not in a pure form or it was dynamic. It had fallen into a corpus, kind of a waste product, and that waste product clogged the dynamic. So Paracelsus taught that in order to bring it back into a dynamic state, I would have to take it apart and purify each part separately. And then recombine it again according to planetary positions. When I do that in a rhythm that is in sync with planetary movements, the substance will marry again in an alchemical marriage at a much higher order of dynamics because the feces have been taken out.

Because I have a consciousness of how to do this, I am part of the tenth hierarchy: I change substance. I can change what the Father God has presented to me through fiat. I cook my burger, which is not natural unless you are scavenging after a volcano.

Whenever you do anything like that, that is not the original creation; you are performing an alchemical process. Roast your coffee beans and pour water through them. Is it French press, or is it pour over, is it drip: it is all alchemy. Taking a substance apart and putting it back together is the great spagyric principle of the alchemical world and that is the essence of the work in Holy Week. Christ is taking apart the old mysteries and purifying each one. By cursing the fig tree and casting the dove sellers out of the temple, He is going through the process. The old mysteries led to the Pharisees where everything was controlled by the law. If you didn't abide by the law, then someone would turn you in.

So the taking apart needs to be done in the way in which it came together. You don't just tell the Father God to take a hike. You have to study the way in which the Father God put it together so that you can take it apart without violating the fundamental principle of life that brought it together in the first place. This is alchemy.

So in the diagram in the figure, we have a bunch of plants in a hermetic vessel. We have water with fire underneath. If you set up that apparatus and you get the fire and water going, the steam goes through the plants. The water is collected and the oil that was in the plant forms a little film as a distillate on the surface of the water. The distillate means that something that was a fixed substance has been lifted to a higher form and then gathered. And the higher form leaves the corpus, the feces or the shadow behind. That is a fundamental principle of alchemy; taking apart a substance so I can liberate it from its fallen element; from the element that prevents it from being more dynamic, more healing.

So I get the oil in part *a*. Then in part *b*, I take what's left over. Put it in water. I put a little yeast and sugar in there and make a wine out of what the plant used to be. In part *c*, I put the wine into a vessel. I light the fire under it (under the earth) and the alcohol comes out of the wine and leaves the feces of the wine.

That alcohol is a much higher level of dynamic activity. Why? If you leave the dish of alcohol out, it will go back into an alcohol spirit. They used to say "Go to the spirits store to get your Jim Beam". They were distilled spirits – such a picture!

Alcohol was considered to be the universal spirit of all plants. So in part c, I take the alcohol off, but then I'm left with what came out of the fermenting in part b. In part d, I put it into a vessel and burn it to ash, but because I've boiled it and steamed it and fermented it, all the cells in the plant are open. And when I dry it, there is a very fine salt released from the ash. The salt is the portion of the plant that drew the water for growth to begin with. That is potassium carbonate. The salt was hidden in all of these processes because it was clogged by the oil and by all of the substances. I lead it through a ritual death, dismembering it and put it into a crucible – a crucifixion fire – in order to release the salt. In alchemy the salt is what in esoteric language Rudolf Steiner calls the phantom. Christ says, "Ye are the salt of the Earth."

This process of trying to get the salt out in a spagyric process is an analogue of the work done on the soul on Monday of Holy Week. The cursing of the fig tree was the opening of the door to the new clairvoyance through personal transformation of the parts of our soul that we are not particularly proud of. This is the shadow and the double which is the feces in our garment. It is the "fallenness" of this force which comes from, in Rudolf Steiner's language, the fall of the spirits of darkness. The picture he gives there is that out of fiat comes this dynamic of the Creator and the created. It's a separation.

There is a separation of the intent of the creator from the evolution of the creation. In the beginning with the Holy Rishis it was, "Yeah, that creation, it's just an image of something but it's not the real deal – don't even worry about it. That's maya." But it was understood that it would be necessary because the creation was going in that direction, it was eventually going to reach a spot where the creation would separate itself from the Creator. The creation would become so dense that it would no longer have any relationship to the divine. That was a problem. If you read in *The Fall of the Spirits of Darkness*, it was a seed that was set in what Steiner calls Old Saturn, a very early evolutionary phase of consciousness that was purely spiritual, of the life of the hierarchies which were participating in the creation.

So there was fiat, and then the Holy Spirit, but in the process of coming down and handing off the fiat from one hierarchy to the next hierarchy, and then to the next hierarchy – a very ancient teaching – that there were different levels of being, that eventually come closer to a manifestation that is sense-perceptible. The issue for this creation was that there was an impulse for fiat to create a being that would have the potential to be separate from the creation. The reason why that was necessary is freedom. There is a famous quote from Goethe, "What would a god be who only pushed things around from the outside?" The answer is that it would be a pretty fundamentalist god just pushing the creation around. "This is the way it is. Just get in line."

As that creation came down, it became a kind of problem for the hierarchies because they kept passing on the idea that eventually there would be a separation, until it came down to the hierarchy that Rudolf Steiner called the Archai, the spirits of personality. The spirits of personality, according to Steiner's esoteric research, had an inner experience that when they had a sensation, the sensation separated them from the object of their sensation. Prior to that, in the hierarchies, the sensation was a mirroring of the sensation and a praise for having the experience of the sensation, back to the Father. The original plan was that there would be an impulse of fiat, and a recognition of the impulse of fiat, "Hosanna in excelsis deo." Praise and glory for the creator!

That was the original plan but there was some small print in the contract that they would forget: "in excelsis deo." It wouldn't be "Thank you for giving me my eyes and my ears." It would be "Hey, what's that out there?" That shift would be the basis of personality. From gratitude for such a miracle to "Hey, this is mine!" That experience of the shifting is the corpus. That's the corpse in the soul, the residue of positivism. And the positivism is "Everything out there is separate from me. I'm going to try and gather as much of it as I can because that is what the game is about." Because it is all about what is here right now. And who is right and who is wrong, and who wins.

That process is what is called the fall. The gist of the fall is that my senses today, the way they are organized, do not allow me to see the action of the divine in the world unless I change them. When I change them, then that is the new clairvoyance.

In order to do that, I have to take images from the world and transform them into metaphors for my inner development. That's what we just did with burning a bunch of plants. It's a symbol or a metaphor for self-transformation. Basically, that is alchemy.

Alchemy is "I take what is in the world and transform it into a symbol of my apotheosis; my path back to the divine."

Glyph for Tuesday – Precipitation

Precipitation

What we are going to do is reproduce the glyph inwardly. Draw it however you wish. This is the glyph for precipitation. Precipitation is that I have a solution of something, I put salt into water and heat it, and the salt disappears from my sense experience. It goes into a solution where it becomes invisible. If I evaporate the water, the salt reappears again in the form that it was in when it disappeared. The forming of a salt out of a solution is precipitation. The dissolving of the salt into a medium like water through warmth is a kind of distillation. That is the "tick tock".

We see precipitation at first as a steady state. Usually a horizontal line in an alchemical equation means the surface of a liquid. This is precipitation and there's a surface of the liquid, and in the liquid there's another kind of surface and then something falls out. If you were reading an alchemical formula and they had that symbol there, you would know that the next thing you would need to do is make a precipitate out of that solution and there are ways to do that with various processes.

For a couple of minutes now, I'm going to ask you to reproduce the form inwardly. You can redraw it over and over until you have a feeling that you are involved with it. Another way is to imagine while you're drawing it, some kind of precipitate, something falling out of a solution as you draw it.

If you really want to get energetic with this, then draw the symbol, the glyph, and then erase it in the opposite order of how you drew it. When you do that, your consciousness participates in the movement of the symbol and you are performing an alchemy by lifting the symbol away from its corpus. You're entering into its dynamic.

We are going to play with this because it is a key element of the work.

Do that for five minutes with the precipitation glyph however you want to do it. You can do it with your finger. You can just do it inwardly. You can draw it on paper. It's up to you.

Now refer to the lower left of the Tree of Knowledge image (next page), where it says "study" within the dotted downward pointing triangle. Let that part of the image be the focus of the crucible. Remember only to ask questions without making comments or statements.

II. Monday

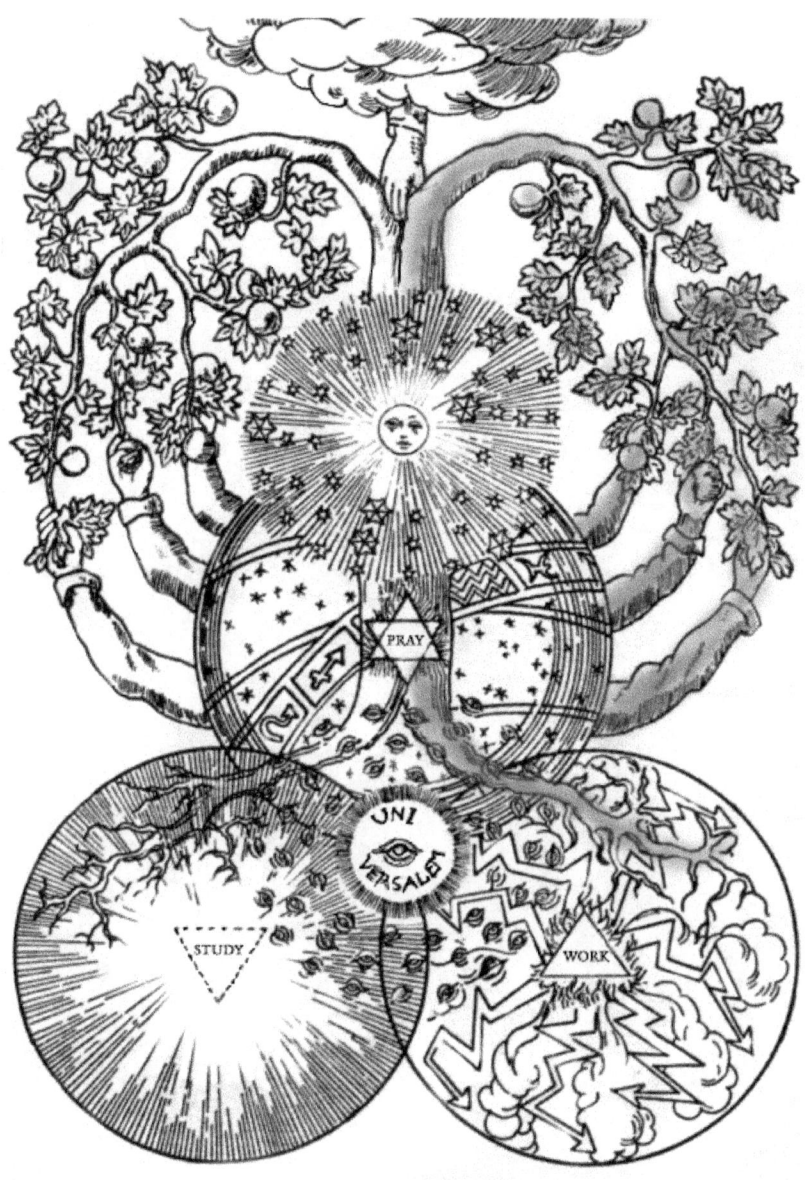

TUESDAY - Judgement and Apocalypse

Luke 17:20-21 Once, on being asked by the Pharisees when the kingdom of God would come, Jesus replied, "The coming of the kingdom of God is not something that can be observed, nor will people say, 'Here it is,' or 'There it is,' because the kingdom of God is in your midst."

Matthew 23:13-32 "Woe to you, teachers of the law and Pharisees, you hypocrites! You shut the door of the kingdom of heaven in people's faces. You yourselves do not enter, nor will you let those enter who are trying to.

"Woe to you, teachers of the law and Pharisees, you hypocrites! You travel over land and sea to win a single convert, and when you have succeeded, you make them twice as much a child of hell as you are.

"Woe to you, blind guides! You say, 'If anyone swears by the temple, it means nothing; but anyone who swears by the gold of the temple is bound by that oath.' You blind fools! Which is greater: the gold, or the temple that makes the gold sacred? You also say, 'If anyone swears by the altar, it means nothing; but anyone who swears by the gift on the altar is bound by that oath.' You blind men! Which is greater: the gift, or the altar that makes the gift sacred? Therefore, anyone who swears by the altar swears by it and by everything on it. And anyone who swears by the temple swears by it and by the one who dwells in it. And anyone who swears by heaven swears by God's throne and by the one who sits on it.

"Woe to you, teachers of the law and Pharisees, you hypocrites! You give a tenth of your spices — mint, dill and cumin. But you have neglected the

more important matters of the law — justice, mercy and faithfulness. You should have practiced the latter, without neglecting the former. You blind guides! You strain out a gnat but swallow a camel. Woe to you, teachers of the law and Pharisees, you hypocrites! You clean the outside of the cup and dish, but inside they are full of greed and self-indulgence. Blind Pharisee! First clean the inside of the cup and dish, and then the outside also will be clean.

"Woe to you, teachers of the law and Pharisees, you hypocrites! You are like whitewashed tombs, which look beautiful on the outside but on the inside are full of the bones of the dead and everything unclean. In the same way, on the outside you appear to people as righteous but on the inside you are full of hypocrisy and wickedness.

"Woe to you, teachers of the law and Pharisees, you hypocrites! You build tombs for the prophets and decorate the graves of the righteous. And you say, 'If we had lived in the days of our ancestors, we would not have taken part with them in shedding the blood of the prophets.' So you testify against yourselves that you are the descendants of those who murdered the prophets. Go ahead, then, and complete what your ancestors started!

Luke 20:1-8 (Tuesday — battle with the Pharisees) One day as Jesus was teaching the people in the temple courts and proclaiming the good news, the chief priests and the teachers of the law, together with the elders, came up to him. "Tell us by what authority you are doing these things," they said. "Who gave you this authority?" He replied, "I will also ask you a question. Tell me: John's baptism — was it from heaven, or of human origin?" They discussed it among themselves and said, "If we say, 'From heaven,' he will ask, 'Why didn't you believe him?' But if we say, 'Of human origin,' all the people will stone us, because they are persuaded that John was a prophet." So they answered, "We don't know where it was from." Jesus said, "Neither will I tell you by what authority I am

III. Tuesday

doing these things."

Luke 21:5-28 (The little apocalypse) Some of his disciples were remarking about how the temple was adorned with beautiful stones and with gifts dedicated to God. But Jesus said, "As for what you see here, the time will come when not one stone will be left on another; every one of them will be thrown down." "Teacher," they asked, "when will these things happen? And what will be the sign that they are about to take place?" He replied: "Watch out that you are not deceived. For many will come in my name, claiming, 'I am he,' and, 'The time is near.' Do not follow them. When you hear of wars and uprisings, do not be frightened. These things must happen first, but the end will not come right away." Then he said to them: "Nation will rise against nation, and kingdom against kingdom. There will be great earthquakes, famines and pestilences in various places, and fearful events and great signs from heaven. But before all this, they will seize you and persecute you. They will hand you over to synagogues and put you in prison, and you will be brought before kings and governors, and all on account of my name. And so you will bear testimony to me. But make up your mind not to worry beforehand how you will defend yourselves. For I will give you words and wisdom that none of your adversaries will be able to resist or contradict. You will be betrayed even by parents, brothers and sisters, relatives and friends, and they will put some of you to death. Everyone will hate you because of me. But not a hair of your head will perish. Stand firm, and you will win life. When you see Jerusalem being surrounded by armies, you will know that its desolation is near. Then let those who are in Judea flee to the mountains, let those in the city get out, and let those in the country not enter the city. For this is the time of punishment in fulfillment of all that has been written. How dreadful it will be in those days for pregnant women and nursing mothers! There will be great distress in the land and wrath against this people. They will fall by the sword and will be taken as prisoners to all the nations. Jerusalem will be trampled on by the Gentiles until the times of the Gentiles are fulfilled. There will be signs in the sun, moon and stars. On the earth, nations will be in anguish and perplexity at the roaring and tossing of the sea. People will faint from terror, apprehensive of what is coming on the world, for the heavenly bodies will be shaken. At that time they will see the Son of Man coming in a cloud with power and great glory. When these things begin to take place, stand up and lift up your heads, because your redemption is drawing near."

Luke 18:1-8 (The Parable of the Persistent Widow) Then Jesus told his disciples a parable to show them that they should always pray and not give up. He said: "In a certain town there was a judge who neither feared God nor cared what people thought. And there was a widow in that town who kept coming to him with the plea, 'Grant me justice against my adversary.' For some time he refused. But finally he said to himself, 'Even though I don't fear God or care what people think, yet because this widow keeps bothering me, I will see that she gets justice, so that she won't eventually come and attack me!' And the Lord said, "Listen to what the unjust judge says. And will not God bring about justice for his chosen ones, who cry out to him day and night? Will he keep putting them off? I tell you, he will see that they get justice, and quickly. However, when the Son of Man comes, will he find faith on the earth?"

Luke 18:9-14 (The Parable of the Pharisee and the Tax Collector) To some who were confident of their own righteousness and looked down on everyone else, Jesus told this parable: "Two men went up to the temple to pray, one a Pharisee and the other a tax collector. The Pharisee stood by himself and prayed: 'God, I thank you that I am not like other people – robbers, evildoers, adulterers – or even like this tax collector. I fast twice a week and give a tenth of all I get.' "But the tax collector stood at a distance. He would not even look up to heaven, but beat his breast and said, 'God,

III. Tuesday

have mercy on me, a sinner.' I tell you that this man, rather than the other, went home justified before God. For all those who exalt themselves will be humbled, and those who humble themselves will be exalted."

On Tuesday of Holy Week there is a lot going on. Monday is the cursing of the fig tree; Tuesday is when there is a kind of turning. Tuesday is Mars day. Mars is aggression and war. The war here is a war of words that Christ was having with the Pharisees because he was out in the countryside preaching and healing, and cutting into the energy of the Pharisees by questioning many of their laws. He was healing on Saturdays, which was not permitted. That was a big deal. Here was an upstart claiming to be the Son of God and healing people. In those days, healing was accepted as the way that prophets established their "street cred" so to speak. In *The Three Years* by Emil Bock, the first chapter is about Apollonius of Tyana, a remarkable clairvoyant and healer at the time of Christ, who was a more prolific healer even than Christ. However as well as being a healer and a prophet, Christ was speaking about things that tied into an insurrection that was fomenting among the common people against Roman rule and the rule of the Pharisees. This was not what Apollonius of Tyana was doing. He was a kind of miracle worker but Christ was fomenting a revolution.

On Tuesday of Holy Week this comes to a head as Christ is in Jerusalem and he is teaching. The Pharisees and scribes come around him and start asking questions, trying to play "gotcha". They had their own spies who were out in the crowds, saying, "He's healing on Saturdays. He is talking against the teachings." and so on. So they were trying to trip him up to make him appear untruthful when he was teaching in front of the people. They were speaking out of a kind of practical tradition of "This is what the rule is." Christ answers them, "But you are not talking about the kingdom of heaven, you are not talking about the Son of Man. You're talking about the stuff that is already past and I'm here to change it." That's the seed for this.

So He is in the temple teaching.

Reading from St. Luke: Once on being asked by the Pharisees when the kingdom of God would come, Jesus replied the coming of the kingdom of God is not something that can be observed. It's not this fixed thing. It is not what you think it is. ...nor will people say 'Here it is,' or 'There it is,' because the kingdom of God is in your midst. The kingdom of God is within you.

That was a total smack in the face to the Pharisees who were all about coming to the temple to buy a dove so that you could be saved. Saying that the kingdom of God is within you: that was insurrection.

In Matthew 23, there are the "woe to you" sayings. This is a thumb in the eye to the Pharisees. "*Woe to you teachers of the law and Pharisees. You hypocrites. You shut the door to the kingdom of heaven in people's faces.*" He is calling a spade a spade here, in the temple. He's prodding the bull. It's really fierce. "You clean the outside of the cup." That was one of the cleanliness laws of the Pharisees. If you are going to drink something you have to clean the outside of the cup, and Christ responds that you first need to clean the inside of the cup so that the outside will be clean. He is speaking about the soul. This is fierce language; he's in the temple and they try to trip Him up and He turns and blasts them. This is when the Pharisees and scribes had all these spies and they would go back and report on what they heard.

There was a religious foment, and as I said earlier, there was a political foment. At this time, because of Roman law and Hebrew law, the common people were expecting the Son of David, the savior, to take care of the Romans. This plays right into the mind of Judas Iscariot. This is kind of apocalyptic. There was an expectation that the apocalypse was going to happen. Roman law would be thrown off, and the scribes and Pharisees would be put in their place. And here was Christ who was performing miracles and prophesying, saying, "Woe to the scribes and Pharisees for they are hypocrites." This is the setting in which Judas will eventually let Satan enter. There is a doorway here, politically and religiously, in Holy Week about a lot of the practices.

The reference to mint, dill and cumin, that is tithing. Ten per cent of what you make is donated. I was talking to a tax lawyer and he said, "You wouldn't think this would be the case but the people who get audited the most are the people who tithe." Because it is an easy way to scam. I give 10% of what I make to the church automatically and then there are all kinds of kickback schemes. So if you really want to get audited, claim 10% tithing to the church, and that's a red flag in the computers of the IRA. That is what Christ is talking about here. They would give 10% of the spices for part of the taxes they owe to the church. This is like a 501(3)(c) arrangement, a kind of tax exempt charitable donation, for the Pharisees.

In Luke, Christ is teaching in the temple courtyards and proclaiming the good news. They come up and ask him by what authority He is doing these things. "Who gives you the authority to say these things?" And He says, "I will also ask you a question. John's baptism – was it from heaven? Or was it of human origin?" This is a big deal because John was baptizing and setting the stage for Christ to come and do this work. The baptism of John was based on something called "metanoia". In the training that was done before baptism, it was understood that baptism would give you metanoia. The derivation of the word is that meta refers to the pole in the circus around which the chariots turned. Noia means "nous" or consciousness. So metanoia means to change the way that your soul thinks about things. This was the foundation of John the Baptist's teaching. He was beheaded, martyred, for teaching metanoia.

Metanoia means: I can think for myself. I'm not thinking what the Scribes and Pharisees are thinking. I have my own thinking that is outside of fundamental dogma. I make up my own mind.

And it was understood that when you had the baptism you became a free individual. This was not a happy idea for the establishment – to have a bunch of free thinkers running around. You go back to Plato. Get rid of the artists and poets because they are insurrectionists and you will be safe.

So He was asking them, "Is that metanoia from the baptism of John from heaven? Or was it made up by John the Baptist as a human?" Luke says they discussed among themselves. "If we say it is from heaven, then He will ask why didn't we believe Him? But if we say it is from human origin, then the people will stone us because they are persuaded that John is a prophet." So they got caught in their own game. They played cat and mouse with Him all of the time. So they answered, "We don't know where it is from." Then He said to them then neither will I tell you where my authority is from.

So that is the mood of this. If we relate this to the crucible, this is study and the mood of study. Does it yield information? Does it

III. Tuesday

yield knowledge? Or does it yield wisdom?

The whole issue of metanoia is changing knowledge into wisdom. To change my thinking about what I know, in order to be able to know that which I think, is impossible to know. I change the way I form my question in order to allow my soul to assimilate lessons that it is destined to assimilate. I have to get rid of systems of knowledge that are already pre-formed in order to allow the spirit to move me.

He was setting the stage for the apostles to go out and preach after He passes away. He was setting the stage for the apostles to believe that He could rise from the dead. He was setting the stage for the apostles to have the experience that no matter what they say, everyone will understand them. And that it's possible to have the experience that if you die before you die, then you will not die when you die.

That is metanoia. He is speaking about the Son of Man, about the eternal part of the human being. Far in the future, the new mysteries will more and more be about having to redeem the corpus of the old mysteries – the precipitate of knowledge that became the law of the Pharisees. What Moses taught and what Abraham taught became a corpse. It was very good when it originated in the Old Testament because it gave the people direction. But by the time it evolved into the law of the Pharisees and scribes, it became tradition bound and fundamentalist. It didn't allow for the growth of wisdom in the people because it was based just on knowledge of the law. All you have to do is memorize the law and you're saved. In certain parts of the world, there are whole portions of real estate being taken over by people who will tell you how you should look, and what you should say when you pray. And if you don't do that, they will kill you. That is fundamentalism squared.

This is with us today, and it is still problematic. Is it knowledge or is it wisdom? There are two kinds of faith: dogmatic faith, and faith that is authentic or you can call it undogmatic. Dogmatic faith is "You must believe because you will never be able to know." That is the faith of the Pharisees. Just memorize this and you will be saved.

Authentic faith is that you believe because you experienced something. The early Christian martyrs had authentic faith because they experienced the movement of the spirit. So they knew that even if the body was killed, they would not be killed. They had authentic faith because they were still very close to the enthusiasm of the metanoia. They got it, and were filled with that experience. They were charismatic. But eventually charisma can also become dogmatic and based on scripture.

What I'm doing here is bringing the scripture, but it's always a symbol, it's not the literal translation of the scripture. It's your experience inwardly of the joy of it, of the metanoia of it, of the potential of it to bring newness into your life, which is what all of the religions talk about. But they give it predigested and programmed no matter what it is. That is the fundamentalist gesture.

In the morning in the temple He deals with the scribes and the Pharisees. Then He goes up to the olive grove on the Mount of Olives. As it's getting close to the time when things will really start to happen, He tells them something known as the Little Apocalypse, and you can read it above in Luke, 21. In that section, He says nation will go against nation and kingdom against kingdom. You will be put into prison and brought before kings and governors. But there is a key right there in Luke 21:14. *But make up your mind not to worry beforehand how you will defend yourselves.*

This is the nature of the new mysteries. Do not think beforehand that knowledge of the scripture is going to save you. Do not think beforehand that what you know of Me is going to save you. But meditate, without answers. Keep your mind free of thinking that you know. And if you do, He says, *"For I will give you words and wisdom that none of your adversaries will be able to resist or contradict. You will be betrayed even by parents, by brothers and sisters, relatives and friends, and they will put some of you to death."* This is not physical death, they will try to kill your spirit with their fundamentalism.

"Everyone will hate you because of Me." Because of what I'm bringing you. I'm bringing you freedom. *"But not a hair of your head will perish. Stand firm and you will win life."* Eternal life in spirit. Just understand that you must give up thinking that you are expected to have the answers, and you will have the answers. I will be there because you will have cleaned your garment and prepared your house for me to come and have dinner. This is fierce.

Let's go to verse 25:

"There will be signs in the sun, moon, and stars. On the earth, nations will be in anguish and perplexity at the roaring and tossing of the sea. People will faint from terror, apprehensive of what is coming on the world, for the heavenly bodies will be shaken. They will see the Son of Man coming in a cloud with power and great glory."

Not the Son of God, the Son of Man. *"When these things begin to take place, stand up and lift up your heads, because your redemption is drawing near."* The Son of Man is the soul, the Sophia—the sophianic vessel of a soul that has been purified of fear and desire and anger and expectation. That is his continual message: that the Son of Man will come. I am the Son of God, I've already come and they are going to trash Me, but now it is your work that needs to move this further.

Rudolf Steiner has a whole series of lectures on something called the new Isis. He describes in those lectures how the Christ event which we are describing here in Holy Week brought the phantom into the Earth. It created a seed for the new Jerusalem. We don't have to search for the Christ, He is the spirit of the Earth. It has already happened. He is already here but it doesn't mean that all you have to do is memorize things and you will be saved. That is not what it means. Steiner says that is a problem. In those Isis lectures, Steiner says that instead we have to search for the new Isis. In the myth of Isis, she was searching for Osiris because he was broken into pieces. He was broken into fragments through the treachery of his brother. He was the chosen one until he got caught up in his drama. So Isis/Osiris is a presaging of Holy Week.

And then Christ becomes the spirit of the Earth. Well, what are we supposed to be doing then if Christ is the spirit of the Earth? We have to search for the broken Christ, who is now the spirit of the Earth — the search for the new Isis. And the search for the new Isis is the search for the eternal feminine, the search for the Sophia, the search for the purified soul force that allows us to transcend desire. That is the new mystery. Hidden in these texts of the New Testament is this gospel of the new mystery — the Son of Man.

After the apocalypse, people will see the Son of Man coming, and say, "What is that?" The people who have been working to create the Son of Man in their souls, will say, "This is the deal!" And the deal is that there is no blame, even for being really stupid.

The gesture here is do not think that in your meditation, you will know the answer. But meditate and pray. Because in the meditation, and the prayer, and in becoming silent, you will be touching the hem of the mystery, participating in the search for the new Isis.

After the Little Apocalypse, the gospels describe parables that Christ gave. I just included a few parables about the Son of Man so you could get a flavor of what this really means.

After mixing it up with the Pharisees, it is pretty clear that something is going to happen. His message is that the Son of Man is where it is at, and the Son of God has to die. This is the Parable of the Persistent Widow (Luke 18:1-8). I'm reading these to you to point to the difference between reading something literally, and reading it symbolically as a gesture towards the Son of Man.

Then Jesus told his disciples a parable to show them that they should always pray and not give up. Pray unceasingly. Pray but don't pray for anything specific. Don't pray that your neighbor will finally shut his dog up — just pray.

In a certain town there was a judge who neither feared God nor cared what people thought. And there was a widow in that town who kept coming to him with the plea, 'Grant me justice against my adversary.' For some time he refused. But finally he said to himself, 'Even though I don't fear God or care what people think, yet because this widow keeps bothering me, I will see that she gets justice, so that she won't eventually come and attack me!' And the Lord said, "Listen to what the unjust judge says. And will not God bring about justice for his chosen ones, who cry out to him day and night? Will he keep putting them off? I tell you, he will see that they get justice, and quickly. However, when the Son of Man comes, will he find faith on the earth?"

Faith — authentic faith — comes once I have the experience that the spiritual world is real. It is not a teaching, not a dogma, but an experience of compassion and caring for others, being willing to serve others. That is the teaching of the new mysteries for freedom: what goes around, comes around. What I put out will come back to me.

This parable sounds a bit weird — about judges and so on — but it is really about the Son of Man. It is about what happens on Earth when the final judgment comes around: the judgment will be made by us. Because, as St. Augustine said, we will be in the imitation of Christ. That is a famous phrase, and also the title of a book by Thomas à Kempis.

So the gesture here in the parable is not about a judge and a widow. Christ is saying, "Look at this judge. He is just doing this because he wants to get her off his back so she doesn't bring a lawsuit against him." He is saying to his disciples, "Think about the Father in heaven. If you get that right with yourself, who is going to judge you?" And when the Son of Man comes, he will say, "You will judge not, lest you be judged." This is tolerance.

The parable of the Pharisee and the tax collector (Luke 18:9-14) is another example. There are many, many of these. If you read them as about the Son of Man, they are kind of funny. If you read them literally, they are about tax collection and money, and it gets very confusing especially if you look at some of the websites by scholars on this parable. It gets a little strange because they are reading it literally, in terms of jurisprudence. But it is not about jurisprudence, it is about the Son of Man.

To some who were confident of their own righteousness and looked down on everyone else, Jesus told this parable:

This is a fundamentalist parable.

"Two men went to the temple to pray, one a Pharisee and the other a tax collector. The Pharisee stood by himself and prayed: 'God, I thank you God that I am not like other people – robbers, evildoers and adulterers – or even like this tax collector. I fast twice a week and give one tenth of all that I get.' But the tax collector stood at a distance. He would not even look up to heaven when he prayed, but beat his breast and said, 'God have mercy on me, a sinner.' I tell you that this man rather than the other went home justified before God. For all of those who exalt themselves will be humbled. And those who humble themselves will be exalted."

In distillation in alchemy, there is the spagyric process which we can see in our diagram. In figure *a* (see below), we have the extraction of oil through distillation. In *b*, the fermentation process which creates wine. In *c*, the separation of the wine from the alcohol in the wine. In *d*, burning what is left over to create an ash. In *e*, I put ash in water and heat the water. What comes out of the ash into the water is the salt that was part of the life process of the plant to begin with.

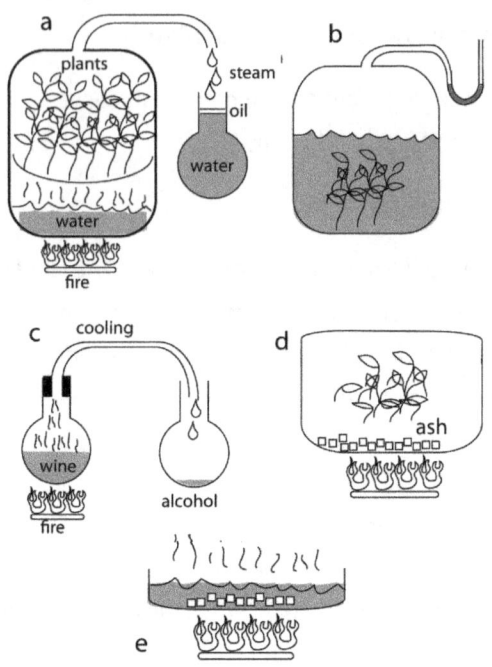

In the growth of a plant there are the salts, potassium and magnesium, which draw water. There are some electrolytic charges within the sap of the plant to make minerals and metals available for growth processes. For the energy a plant needs in order to assimilate sunlight and change it into sugar, there is a series of metals: lithium, potassium, magnesium, sodium and calcium. There is a sequence where they hand off charges to one another that allows for something to pass across membranes. We call it nutrition. Basically it is charges between metals that move from inside a cell, to outside a cell, to inside a cell. In every cell, there are pumps, magnesium pumps, potassium pumps, and a selectively permeable membrane and there is all this chemistry between the inside and the outside of the cell that has to do with metals. That is why the alchemists were so interested in metals. And the metals are in the form of salts: potassium salts, magnesium salts. If they were in their original form, they would be toxic but when they form a salt, they become benign. Within the blood, the relation between potassium and calcium salts is an exchange of fluid into a cell, and out of a cell: this is nutrition and excretion. This is just the chemistry of the blood, through salt.

When a plant is formed, the substance of the plant is salt, metals that have been configured by light, sunlight. Photosynthesis: photo – light – synthesis. What is it synthesizing? Metals. The plant is a supreme alchemist.

Through this whole process, the goal is to get the salt. The salt is the precipitate of life. It forms out of life as an image of how life comes from the spiritual world into manifestation, and goes back again. I take salt, I put it in water. I heat the water, the salt disappears. Where did it go? Now, I evaporate the water and the salt comes back again. This would be seen by an alchemist as an analogue of the whole process of incarnation and excarnation. They call it the living salt. You get, "Ye are the salt of the Earth." So the forming of the salt, a precipitate, is a kind of abstract of the processes that were going on in the plant using the salt to create forms.

In the realm of the inner life of the soul, the thought that we form is the salt of the process of the thinking that we are doing. The word that you hear is just the salt of the possible words that I could say. The alchemist would say that the word that you hear is a salt or corpse of the Word.

The note that you hear in music is the salt of the energy in the music. It is not the music; it is the death of the music. The music is how your soul stretches from the fundamental to the octave and back again. That is how the soul hears music. Back in the day, it was not written down, it was just played or sung, so your soul could participate in it. Now, it is little dots on a piece of paper – and you had better play it the right way or you won't get asked back to the competition any more. It is the corpse of it.

I see that the difference between the salt and the ash is the central mystery of alchemy, after studying it for forty years. There have been entire alchemical books written about the salt. James Hillman spent his career writing about the alchemical salt: a dead thing that attracts life.

The most dead part of me is the part that is of most interest to Angels because they don't understand it. My corpse is like graduate school for Angels. They wonder, "What is that? Why are you so attached to it?" They don't get it, because they don't have the potential for freedom unless we become free. Being an Angel is a hard job description because they have to get these stupid humans to wake up.

So the forming of the salt is like the knowledge of the Pharisees that came out of the wisdom of Abraham. By the time Christ needed to come back, the wisdom of Abraham was a corpse. It was just a bunch of stuff that had been written and it was being used to subjugate the people. And He came back to say, "This is not what my Father had in mind, Pharisees making book on the common people in my Father's name, so I need to come back and change this." The people said, "He is back, and He is going to whack the Romans and the Pharisees, and we're all going to have a free

III. Tuesday

ticket to ride. He is going to tell us what to do and it will all be OK."

Christ said, "I am not going to tell you what to do. I am just going to tell you stories and you can take them how you will. Here is a story about a judge and a widow – what do you think?"

When you interpret them literally, it becomes what is called exegesis: what does it mean? But if you take it as a symbolic language, as an alchemical, metaphoric language, then He is speaking about the future human, the Son of Man. Christ's mission is to awaken people to their own divinity. Not the divinity that was already described, but how you experience life in this incredible vehicle. You begin to realize that you will be given another upgrade sometime, and so we get to Steiner's mission, and we can look at Christian Rosenkreutz as a vehicle for Mani. The Rosicrucian material that I am speaking about is the middle of the Oreo cookie. It is not the end game. The whole issue of where this process is going has to do with the phantom. On Tuesday of Holy Week, we have these stories and the apocalypse, and sticking a finger in the eye.

We get to the place where the study of the ancient books has led to a very fixed salt. The whole issue of the alchemists is what is known as dealbation: the purifying of the salt. The way you purify the salt is when you burn the plant and have the ash and extract the salt from the ash, it is kind of a dull gray. When you put that salt into water and boil it again and the water all goes off, and you look at the salt, it is a little bit lighter. You take the water that has come off, you put it back on. Then you boil it again to take the water off, it's a little lighter still. You keep repeating this process and that's dealbation, the whitening of the salt. In the alchemical language, it's understood that I am loosening the salt from the remnants of the feces through repeated distillation. As I repeat the distillation, the volatilization of the salt in the steam, they used to call it "the widow of steam", would go up and separate from what was below but loosen the impurities and eventually volatilize the salt. When the salt would become volatile, they called the salt "the eagle". The salt has been given wings. They wanted to get the salt to fly over so that eventually it would marry the oil that they took off right at the beginning. The oil you get is an essential oil which, if you leave the cap off, it volatilizes; it just evaporates. They are very volatile, very spiritous.

The salt is gravity laden until I purify it into an eagle. When I purify it into an eagle, it flies over and can marry the oil. The oil is the oil of mercy and we will get there when we get to Good Friday with the whole issue of the oil of mercy that Seth has to travel to find on the path to the redeeming of Adam. It is a whole process of oil. Oil is always fire. It supports combustion. When the oil ignites, there is no ash. It just goes away. I have to get it to marry the salt.

The salt does not want to go away, it wants to form dogma. The salt wants to make a crystallized experience of the divine and put it in a book. This drama here of "Study" (see Tree of Life diagram). The Study has led to the corpus of the Study which is dogma.

When I have dogma, I no longer really have to study because I have the experience that in the dogma, there are already all the answers that I need. Something in me dies. What dies in me is the willingness to live in the unknown, which is just what Christ is telling the apostles they need to do, "Just pray and don't worry about the answer."

The purifying of the salt in consciousness is the repeated

meditative practice. You just have to keep repeating it and doing it in order to make it live, because the only time that it lives is when you do it. Why? Because you are a student, you are a wannabe divinity. It is true. That is what this is about. You are only in the school of divinity when you are praying and in contact with the Son of Man. Then you are a player, otherwise you are on the bench.

Study has led to dogma and hypocrisy. It does not have to do that but that is one picture. In Study (see Tree of Life diagram), the triangle is pointing down. That is earth.

Glyph for Wednesday – Alcohol and Oil

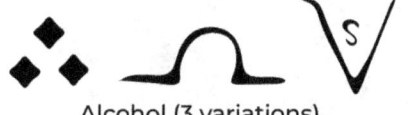
Alcohol (3 variations)

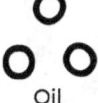
Oil

Alchemy of Holy Week

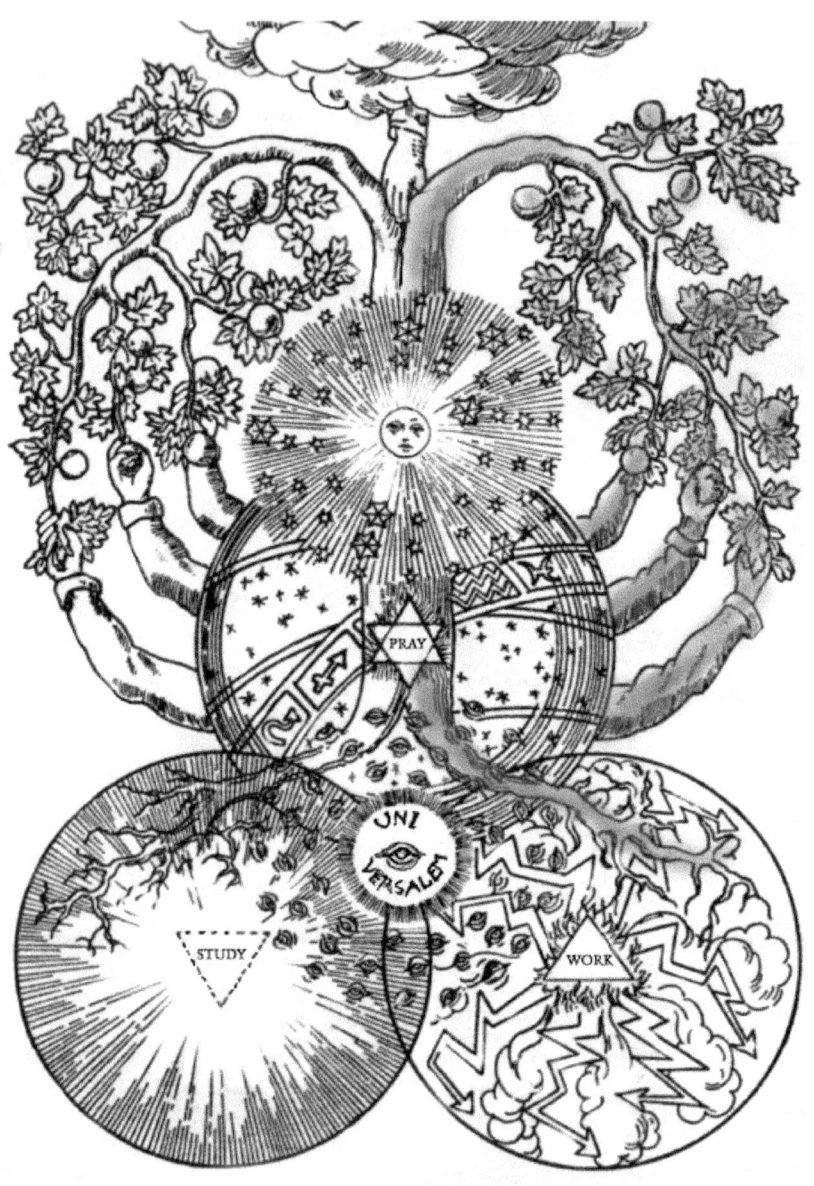

WEDNESDAY - Anointing

Mark 14:1-11 Now the Passover and the Festival of Unleavened Bread were only two days away, and the chief priests and the teachers of the law were scheming to arrest Jesus secretly and kill him "But not during the festival," they said, "or the people may riot."

While he was in Bethany, reclining at the table in the home of Simon the Leper, a woman came with an alabaster jar of very expensive perfume, made of pure nard. She broke the jar and poured the perfume on his head. Some of those present were saying indignantly to one another, "Why this waste of perfume? It could have been sold for more than a year's wages and the money given to the poor." And they rebuked her harshly. "Leave her alone," said Jesus. "Why are you bothering her? She has done a beautiful thing to me. The poor you will always have with you, and you can help them any time you want. But you will not always have me. She did what she could. She poured perfume on my body beforehand to prepare for my burial. Truly I tell you, wherever the gospel is preached throughout the world, what she has done will also be told, in memory of her." Then Judas Iscariot, one of the Twelve, went to the chief priests to betray Jesus to them. They were delighted to hear this and promised to give him money. So he watched for an opportunity to hand him over.

In this session, I will combine Wednesday and Thursday. We will focus on "work" and "pray". Work is in the lower right of the Tree of Life diagram: that is the upward pointing triangle with the lightning bolts. Work is in the upward pointing triangle which represents fire. Pray is in the center of the Star of David on the trunk of the tree with the symbols for the zodiac going through it and the starry realms around it. Those are the two parts we will look at for the crucible.

Wednesday is Mercury's day. Mercury is the great healer; it unites the opposites or separates the opposites. Mercury is the patron of healers and thieves. Things just move; they either get better or they get worse – Mercury doesn't care as long as there is change.

On Mercury day, the gospel reading is about the anointing of the Christ. In this particular excerpt, Mary Magdalene anoints Christ. Some say a woman, but most say Mary Magdalene. This brings up a theme that was present in the ancient world that is still an issue today in parts of the Middle East, and that is the role of women in society, or the role of women in general. This issue is kind of buried in the gospels but it goes back to the time of the gnostics in the 4th and 5th century, when the idea of Sophia as a kind of consort to Christ coming through the hierarchies was a part of gnostic doctrine.

There is a book called the *Pistis Sophia* about the journey of Sophia through the hierarchies, coming from being the wisdom of God to being like a goat or sacrificial animal, descending through the hierarchies until she gets to the 13th hierarchy when she realizes she is separate from the divine and yearns to be back with the divine. She recognizes that the yearning in her has no place in the original creation.

This is the Pistis Sophia. Pistis means faith. Sophia means the wisdom of God. She was an avatar of God the father, the creator. Anthroposophy is permeated by gnostic ideas, in case you are wondering why we would bring that in here. There is so much teaching such as the nine hierarchies, Dionysius the Areopagite and the false Dionysius, that comes from gnostic lore. Steiner also mentions the Pistis Sophia.

Sophia was one with God and then she traveled through the thirteen aeons, as they are called in that lore, the hierarchies. When she gets to the thirteenth one, she realizes she is divorced from the divine, as she has moved all the way through. She had become an avatar of the divine, an aspect of the total divinity – that is what avatar means. She had become an aspect of the wisdom of the divine and has brought that wisdom through the hierarchies for the creation. But then she had become the sacrificial lamb for the creation because she had given over her wisdom to the hierarchies and when she got to the thirteenth she realizes she has bought the package.

She also realizes that the yearning to be one with the divine has no place in the creation, because it was all meant to be simply a reflection of the greater glory of God. She knows that she can't carry that, so she creates an avatar and casts it away. It falls below the original creation, and becomes the Sophia, the faithful Sophia, the Pistis Sophia of the fall, known as the Achamoth. This is the fallen wisdom of the creation becoming knowledge.

She was in the darkness because she no longer had sight of the divine. The way the gnostic doctrine deals with that is that the Christ being, held in abeyance within the Trinity, then followed her down through the creation, and saw that she was bereft of the experience of the divine.

In this story, the Christ being has to travel through the hierarchies because the Sophia wishes to have union with the divine but the other hierarchies have set up a kind of patriarchal force against her. They say that when she came through them, she came from above and just passed on through without honoring their sacrifices. Now they do not want her coming back again. There was this patriarchal issue of the feminine in the creation. It comes from gnostic lore.

This story anticipates the struggle between Saint Peter and Mary Magdalene in the gospel. It is being told to the disciples after Golgotha. Christ comes back and stays with them and teaches them about the fall of Sophia. In the way the story works, the Pistis Sophia laments the fact that she passed through the hierarchies and did not honor their sacrifices. It was also her sacrifice, but it has become complicated because she represents a yearning to transcend Creation.

This is part of the new mysteries, a yearning to get back to God, "Just take my self away from me so I can be one." Carl Jung said the addiction of an alcoholic is the yearning to be one with God. All of our addictions and all of our desires are a yearning to be back in good communication with the divine. The Pistis Sophia represents that as an avatar.

This is the Black Madonna, the one who has gone down and is now suffering in the darkness with the creation. She is down below. Christ travels through, and she has a lament for each hierarchy. As Christ is telling the story to the disciples, He tells them about her laments and for each one He asks, "Who can explain this lament?".

One by one, they answer that it is like the Psalms of David as a parallel to her laments through the hierarchies. And Christ says they have spoken well. But whenever there is a question, Christ turns to Mary Magdalene for confirmation, and asks the apostles why they don't call on this woman. They finally get through but there are thirteen laments and twelve apostles. The thirteenth lament is the big ticket item and none of the apostles can explain it. Mary Magdalene comes forward and explains the thirteenth lament and Christ thanks her.

Then there is a fourteenth lament that is related to the future of the Sophia. We could even call her, with what we know through the genius of Rudolf Steiner, the Anthroposophia. And that being also laments. Christ asks who can explain this. None of the apostles can explain it. Mary Magdalene cannot explain it. Ultimately, it takes the Mother of Jesus to explain it. She does that and then tells them a story about what happened to her before Jesus was born.

So this anointing by the mysterious woman is a very big deal. It is not just a little anecdotal story. It is a picture of a whole movement in the ancient world towards subjugation of the feminine principle. The sacrifice of the feminine principle is to serve as what they called the vessel of God, the one that carries the divine.

That is why Anthroposophia is a feminine being. This is one of the new mysteries — the Marian mystery. I wanted to give you a little background because you can read this and think OK, a woman came and anointed him, and move on. It is a very deep picture of the difference between the old patriarchal mystery, "Get in line or I'll whack you on the head!" and the new feminine mystery, which is "Let's talk."

As soon as I have an opinion of you, I'm putting you down. That's just anger and guilt and shame. And the new mysteries are to heal that by allowing everyone to be as stupid as they can be, because it will all work out. Just pray and don't think that you know the answer.

Reading from the gospel of St. Mark:

Now the Passover and the Festival of Unleavened Bread were only two days away, and the chief priests and the teachers of the law were scheming to arrest Jesus secretly and kill him. "But not during the festival," they said, "or the people may riot."

While he was in Bethany, this is up in Galilee, *reclining at the table in the home of Simon the Leper,* He was fraternizing with lepers, criminals, prostitutes and fishermen, hanging out with losers. The officials would have been dismayed but they didn't understand the new mysteries, where we are all losers.

A woman came with an alabaster jar of very expensive perfume, made of pure nard, which is the herb spikenard, a member of the Valerian family. Valerian is a deep Mercury oil: take too much and it is a stimulant. Take just enough of it and it is one of the best sedatives. If you smell good quality spikenard, it has a deeply ancient, mysterious fragrance, and it was used to anoint the dead.

The woman broke the jar and poured the perfume on His head. She was anointing Him for His death.

Some of those present were saying indignantly to one another, "Why this waste of perfume?" These were his disciples, and some say that this was the beginning of Judas turning, because he was the treasurer of the disciples. He held the purse strings. He criticized the woman saying, *"It could have been sold for more than a year's wages and the money given to the poor." And they rebuked her harshly.* They put her down because she had anointed the Christ to prepare for his death.

"Leave her alone," said Jesus. "Why are you bothering her? She has done a beautiful thing to me. The poor you will always have with you and you

can help them any time you want. But you will not always have me. She did what she could. She anointed my body beforehand to prepare for my burial." They did not understand that He was going to die.

"Truly I tell you, wherever the gospel is preached throughout the world, what she has done will also be told, in memory of her." The whole grail mystery with Joseph of Arimathea and Mary Magdalene comes out of this, and the taking of the true blood from Golgotha in the grail cup. *Then Judas Iscariot, one of the Twelve, went to the chief priests to betray Jesus to them. They were delighted to hear this and promised to give him money. So he watched for an opportunity to hand him over.*

This is a deep Mercury mystery. Mercury consists of the male and female together. In the language of alchemy, it is known as the great hermaphrodite. Very often in alchemy, you will see a picture of someone where one side has female genitalia and the other side has male genitalia and they are together in one person with a common crown. This is the great hermaphrodite and it is also the future Son of Man with the male principle and female principle combined. It is a symbol because it is a union where the spirit and the soul and the body come together. It is the great marriage of the male principle and the female principle within one person.

Coming from the matriarchal times, and the fall of the ancient world where matriarchy held the power, to patriarchal times where power became dogmatic, this now shifts back towards the Marian church.

The American continent was supposed to be the source of the lifting of the seven seals of the book of the Apocalypse. The lifting of the seven seals was to reveal that the future of the church was to be a Marian-based church, the "mother" church, and no longer a Petrine [Peter-based] church.

That was to be on this continent but it got twisted and was scuttled. During the time when this was supposed to happen, there was the apparition of the Virgin of Guadalupe. The place where that vision happened to Juan Diego was believed to be the home of Quetzalcoatl, a sacred site for the Indigenous people of Mexico. It was believed Quetzalcoatl's mother was also a virgin who gave birth to a being who would be sacrificed, which resonated with the story of the Christ. When the Indigenous people learned that the Virgin had come who shared the same story as Quetzalcoatl, they embraced this story. There was also a prophecy that when the Europeans came to this continent, the Virgin would appear and a new church would be started here. That is why the Holy See bankrolled the expedition to the West that led to the founding of the missions and presidios in California and Mexico. It was not about getting the gold, but to bring the Marian church into play. That was to be a new Marian church of the new blood of innocent people.

It was said that at the time of Golgotha, there was a saint, Thomas Quetzalcoatl, who traveled to Mexico and brought news of Golgotha to the Indigenous people to ward off issues that were happening with a black magician. Thomas told them that this prophecy would come when a Christ being would appear to them. That powerful figure would appear to shine and would have fair skin and red hair. It just so happened that when Cortez landed, wearing shining armor and with his pale skin and red hair, they believed that this was the return of Quetzalcoatl because it was predicted by Saint Thomas Quetzalcoatl, but it turned out that it was not the Christ. It was Cortez.

This continent was intended to be a kind of *vas dei*, a vessel for the new mysteries. And it still is, but there is a lot that happened because we remain in the last stages of the Roman empire, definitely not yet the Marian.

When Manfred Schmidt-Brabant came here [to Rudolf Steiner College] years ago, he gave some lectures about California. He said that it is the feminine mysteries that will start here in California and move east. This land is the beginning of the new mystery stream because everything to the east has already happened, but it hasn't quite happened here yet. California is a seed from Lemuria. It is what is left over from Lemuria. There is a small strip of Lemuria left over in Auburn under the railroad bridge. You can read about it in the book *Assembling California*. That strip of shale is the most ancient rock of what was left over from the continent of Cascadia, which used to underlie the whole Pacific Ocean. It melded on to the west coast, and we could say that little strip is the last bit of Lemuria. That has been compressed into some of the oldest deposits here in California. This area with the gold and all of that is a Magdalene, feminine mystery of healing. The woman with the alabaster vase is trying to heal Him, while the men are worried about the bottom line. It is such a picture. Is it the bottom line? Or is it that we are all in this together? We see it in our political life. Can we allow people to come here who are refugees? Shall we allow people who are indigent to have health care? Or can we just not afford it?

So, she is anointing Him with spikenard. The issue with anointing with spikenard in alchemy is that it is an oil. It is always a substance created by a plant as a kind of protection of the embryo. Oils and resins are there to create a condition where the cooking of all of the salt has been lifted only to the finest parts that are highly volatile.

The oil process of Mercury, and the anointing that she performs is the beginning of the separation of the mission of Jesus from the mission of Christ. It began at the baptism, but Emil Bock said that it took a while because Christ was a divine being packed into a physical body. And then He realized that He was going to have to die in this body. This was a turning point towards the Passion.

Wednesday is Mercury day, and we get the splitting of the male and female principles. One is the anointing and the blessing and the protecting, and the other one is the bottom line, and making some money from betraying this person.

The reason why Judas wanted to betray Christ was that he was part of a sect that was deeply political and sought to overthrow Roman rule. He had been around Jesus Christ long enough to know that He had real power, the power to do anything He wanted. So Judas' motive was to push Christ into a spot where he was going to have to use His power to save Himself. Judas wanted to do that by manipulating circumstances, knowing that Christ would have to choose to kill all the soldiers. They could finally instigate a takeover, overthrow Roman rule, and push the Pharisees out of the way. Then Judas could be Chief Financial Officer for the new government. So he was pushing to have that happen. Every step along the way he got a little more tense and a little more tense, until he got to this place where they were blowing money on spikenard oil. He had no idea that there was going to be a crucifixion.

Judas was just pushing and this was a time of great foment in Jerusalem, political foment, religious forment. The common people were agitating. It was like the Arab spring. And Jesus Christ was the flashpoint. So Judas had just had it, and decided to set it into motion. He went to the Pharisees to betray him and told them where Jesus would be, and that He could be arrested on the grounds that He was inciting a riot. They were the charges if you read about Pilate, but it was also connected with Passover and it gets very technical. If you would like more detail, read *The Three Years* by Emil Bock.

So that is Wednesday. He gets anointed.

Glyph for Thursday – Ouroborus

Ouroborus

THURSDAY – Washing of feet

John 13:1-17 It was just before the Passover Festival. Jesus knew that the hour had come for him to leave this world and go to the Father. Having loved his own who were in the world, he loved them to the end. The evening meal was in progress, and the devil had already prompted Judas, the son of Simon Iscariot, to betray Jesus. Jesus knew that the Father had put all things under his power, and that he had come from God and was returning to God; so he got up from the meal, took off his outer clothing, and wrapped a towel around his waist. After that, he poured water into a basin and began to wash his disciples' feet, drying them with the towel that was wrapped around him. He came to Simon Peter, who said to him, "Lord, are you going to wash my feet?" Jesus replied, "You do not realize now what I am doing, but later you will understand." "No," said Peter, "you shall never wash my feet." Jesus answered, "Unless I wash you, you have no part with me." "Then, Lord," Simon Peter replied, "not just my feet but my hands and my head as well!" Jesus answered, "Those who have had a bath need only to wash their feet; their whole body is clean. And you are clean, though not every one of you." For he knew who was going to betray him, and that was why he said not every one was clean. When he had finished washing their feet, he put on his clothes and returned to his place. "Do you understand what I have done for you?" he asked them. "You call me 'Teacher' and 'Lord,' and rightly so, for that is what I am. Now that I, your Lord and Teacher, have washed your feet, you also should wash one another's feet. I have set you an example that you should do as I have done for you. Very truly I tell you, no servant is greater than his master, nor is a messenger greater than the one who sent him. Now that you know these things, you will be blessed if you do them.

On Thursday, the disciples rent a room to celebrate the Passover. Reading from the John gospel: *Jesus knew the hour had come for Him to leave this world and go to his Father.* When Judas decided to act, and Mary Magdalene anointed Him for His burial, that was the beginning of the Passion. *Having loved his own who were in the world, he loved them to the end. The evening meal was in progress, and the devil had already prompted Judas, the son of Simon Iscariot, to betray Jesus. Jesus knew that the Father had put all things under his power, and that he had come from God and was returning to God.* At this point, Jesus is representing the consciousness of the Son of Man. It is not, "You come from dust, and to dust you shall return." That is the Adamic body, but this is, "I come from the Father and I'm going back to the Father." This is the Son of Man.

This is not unique to Christianity because the Indigenous peoples say that we are star people who just visit here to learn how to be limited. This idea is that we are truly transcendent beings, learning the answer to the questions: What does it mean when you die? What does it mean that you are alive? This all hinges on the idea of having a sense experience. We will go there in our next session. Meanwhile, the evening meal is in progress. The devil has already gotten to Judas.

Jesus knew that the Father had put all things under his power, and that he had come from God and was returning to God; so he got up from the meal, took off his outer clothing, and wrapped a towel around his waist. After that, he poured water into a basin and began to wash his disciples' feet...

At this time, everyone wore sandals and walked around on dusty roads. So before you went to the table, you would wash your feet, just as we have a tradition of washing our hands before a meal.

...drying them with a towel that was wrapped around Him. He came to Simon Peter, who said to him, "Lord, Are you going to wash my feet?"

Jesus replied, "You do not realize now what I am doing. But later you will understand."

Christ knew that Peter was to be the foundation of the new church. He also knew that Peter was going to deny that he had any relationship to Christ when the heat came on, and that is what happened.

"No," said Peter, "you shall never wash my feet." Jesus answered, "Unless I wash you, you have no part with me." "Then, Lord," Simon Peter replied, "not just my feet but my hands and my head as well!" Jesus answered, "Those who have had a bath need only to wash their feet; their whole body is clean. And you are clean, though not every one of you."

Christ is not speaking about his Adamic body. He is speaking about his Son of Man body.

Washing feet is essentially asking, "Can I serve you? Can I understand how you feel when I say something to you? Can I awaken something in you out of what I am bringing?" This is washing the feet.

For he knew who was going to betray him, and that was why he said not every one was clean. When he had finished washing their feet, he put on his clothes and returned to his place. "Do you understand what I have done for you?" he asked them. You call me 'Teacher' and 'Lord,' and rightly so, for that is what I am. Now that I, your Lord and Teacher, have washed your feet, you also should wash one another's feet. I have set you an example that you should do as I have done for you. Very truly I tell you, no servant is greater than his master... These are the new mysteries. This is Abraham Lincoln who said, "Not only would I not be a slave, I would not be a master." They crucified him too on Good Friday. *Very truly I tell you, no servant is greater than his master, nor is a messenger greater than the one who sent him. Now that you know these things, you will be blessed if you do them.*

This is the basis of the new mysteries out of the healing of Mercury; the willingness to be awake to the other. Rudolf Steiner calls it "awakening in the other", and he goes on to say that you cannot awaken in another with a concept. You can only awaken in another with a picture, a feeling picture. It is a feeling picture of how the person is responding to what you are bringing to them. This is known as prescience. Prescience means I can feel the soul tone within me as a kind of picture of how this person is receiving what I am bringing to them with my gaze, my tone of voice and my intent, but not my content.

Roman law is about content. The new mysteries are about intent. This gesture of prescience means developing the ability to wash the feet of another. It means I understand what is going on in you when I am saying something to you. And prescience is then the Holy Spirit, the healer who will bring the male and female together by creating inner pictures in me of what is going on in you. That is why you can never awaken anyone else with a concept because it is too abstract. You can only awaken them with a picture of what is going on with them, based on how you are feeling what is going on with them. This is empathy. It is a Marian, feminine mystery. It is not sympathy or antipathy.

These are all code words. Rudolf Steiner said there are two forces in the soul: sympathy and antipathy. Sympathy is a code word for Lucifer. Lucifer is a code word for "This is what is going on in me. I'm going to tell you what I think you need to hear." I have sympathy with myself. Ahriman is gravity. "Sign up for this service, everything is there, you can download it, pay your monthly fee and you can get all the clairvoyance you want." Levity and gravity need to be brought together in Mercury, the great healer who brings the male and female together into the center, into the Christ.

The Christ principle is aware of the degrees of sympathy and antipathy that I am creating in the people around me. Am I getting them to be too sympathetic? Am I getting them to be antipathetic? If I have an opinion about them, I am essentially putting them down.

So on Thursday, after He washes the feet and they eat the meal of the last supper, Judas leaves after the meal. Christ then goes to the Mount of Olives, where he talks to the disciples about staying awake and going to sleep. That is a microcosm of the new mysteries: Can you stay awake with me while I'm going through my trials and tribulations? It's going to happen. Peter says, "I'm with you 100 percent!"

Then Christ has a dialogue with Peter about whether he will deny Him. This is such a picture of how my conditional belief, I could say, is at odds with my unconditional belief. The way a belief works is to put one into a position of unconditional belief. We can call that meditation. My true self, my representative of the Son of Man, with my consciousness completely silent, that is who I will be at the end times. I and so will you, we will all be totally awake with a sense perception for the whole cosmos, with not even the impulse to blog. No reflection, no reaction. Simply sensing the reality of the "I am" of Christ. Christ is "I am".

In the Trinity, the Father God is fiat; the Son God is "I am". When in meditation, we are completely silent, we are "I am". That is who we really are. However, we have a job description that says, "You too will fall." This is because we inherited from Adam and Eve, an Adamic body. The need for the Adamic body is a function of your sense experience, in which you believe that everything in the world has nothing to do with you, except for the things you desire.

Look at the table. Do you desire the table? No, it is just a corpse among other corpses. But now if I ask you to put your credit card on the table, do you desire your credit card? Somebody does. But it's just another thing. That drama of attachment versus non-attachment, intent versus content, comes from having an Adamic body that has been infiltrated by Lucifer and Ahriman to change the way that sense organs work. The sense organs now work in a way that you believe you are the one who is the originator of your thoughts. Rudolf Steiner said that is the most ridiculous thing in the world if you actually thought about it – no pun intended. Or you believe that all the people in this room are totally separate from you. That is another great illusion. When you go to the other side, you become them.

V. Thursday

The drama of the separate self, the illusion of the separate self, is because the original purpose of the senses was to take in sensations in silence and reflect it back in joy. That intention was infiltrated and usurped, firstly by Lucifer who caused the senses to fall. In the gnostic language, the fall of Sophia was due to Lucifer finally seeing her coming through the thirteenth aeon and imprisoning her in his belt of lies.

The appearance of the sense world as separate is Lucifer's hocus pocus. Why does he want us to believe that? So that we won't even go down into the sense world but instead will follow him. This is the basis of the old mysteries. Here, take this, smoke this, drink this, and then get out of the sense world. I'll leave you out there and you will learn things. Those are the Luciferic mysteries. The Ahrimanic mysteries are the vices; they are about the control of power, "There's a cool thing: try this!"

These two have infiltrated the original form of the sense experience with the idea that every thing in the world is separate. You need to understand that this blackboard is this thing and it came into being in a particular way which was its spiritual path, its line of emergence. The patterns of whatever formed it are still present. If I change the way I think about my sense experience of the blackboard, I can begin to see how this part of it was made by an extruder, and this part was actually painted on. If I do that, I start to have an inner experience of how it was made. I experience what bauxite was in Canada before it became aluminum. That is the new clairvoyance because it is cognitive.

Thinking is the basis of the new clairvoyance, because you have to check whatever comes out of your mouth. If you don't, then you are in Ahriman's realm.

If you believe everything in the world is separate, then everything in the world becomes "stuff", because those two beings have infiltrated sense experience in the human being. We are caught in this web of that belief of being separate from everything and needing power to be able to keep what is separate.

In the healing of that, I first have to control my own inner picture. That is why we are using glyphs. I determine the way the picture is built. That is my organ of perception. And then I take that picture that I determined, I move it forwards and backwards, and when I say, "Listen into your heart", that is the doorway to silence. When I learn how to create conditions of silence, I place the pictures that I created into the realm of silence. The beings on the other side of the threshold allow the Christ being to move through them, to say "Here's how the other person is experiencing what you are saying, what you just said, what you look like, what you expect." They are clairvoyant to your intent, so that you are not fooling anybody. It is all this stuff we actually know but we agree we don't know because it becomes uncomfortable if we think we know

The work with glyphs, pictures and symbols, and dissolving them builds an inner capacity to tolerate longer states of silence so that I can find out who I am.

Glyph for Friday – Digestion

Digestion

FRIDAY – Last Supper and Gethsemane

Mark 14:17-37 When evening came, Jesus arrived with the Twelve. While they were reclining at the table eating, he said, "Truly I tell you, one of you will betray me – one who is eating with me." They were saddened, and one by one they said to him, "Surely you don't mean me?" "It is one of the Twelve," he replied, "one who dips bread into the bowl with me. The Son of Man will go just as it is written about him. But woe to that man who betrays the Son of Man! It would be better for him if he had not been born." While they were eating, Jesus took bread, and when he had given thanks, he broke it and gave it to his disciples, saying, "Take it; this is my body." Then he took a cup, and when he had given thanks, he gave it to them, and they all drank from it. "This is my blood of the covenant, which is poured out for many," he said to them. "Truly I tell you, I will not drink again from the fruit of the vine until that day when I drink it new in the kingdom of God." When they had sung a hymn, they went out to the Mount of Olives. "You will all fall away," Jesus told them, "for it is written: 'I will strike the shepherd, and the sheep will be scattered.' But after I have risen, I will go ahead of you into Galilee." Peter declared, "Even if all fall away, I will not." "Truly I tell you," Jesus answered, "today–yes, tonight–before the rooster crows twice you yourself will disown me three times." But Peter insisted emphatically, "Even if I have to die with you, I will never disown you." And all the others said the same. They went to a place called Gethsemane, and Jesus said to his disciples, "Sit here while I pray." He took Peter, James and John along with him, and he began to be deeply distressed and troubled. "My soul is overwhelmed with sorrow to the point of death," he said to them. "Stay here and keep watch." Going a little farther, he fell to the ground and prayed that if possible the hour might pass from him. "Abba, Father," he said, "everything is possible for you. Take this cup from me. Yet not what I will, but what you will." Then he returned to his disciples and found them sleeping. "Simon," he said to Peter, "are you asleep? Couldn't you keep watch for one hour? Watch and pray so that you will not fall into temptation. The spirit is willing, but the flesh is weak."

We will start with the Last Supper and then move on to the garden of Gethsemane.

When evening came, Jesus arrived with the Twelve. While they were reclining at the table eating, he said, "Truly I tell you, one of you will betray me—one who is eating with me." They were saddened, and one by one they said to him, "Surely you don't mean me?" "It is one of the Twelve," he replied, "one who dips bread into the bowl with me. The Son of Man will go just as it is written about him. But woe to that man who betrays the Son of Man!"

Hopefully, the 'Son of Man' means more than it did before you began. We are talking about the future human. The one who betrays the future human will not be happy: "It would be better for him that he not be born." This is about the betrayal of the Son of Man.

"While they were eating, Jesus took bread and when he had given thanks, He broke it and gave it to his disciples, saying, "Take it; this is my body." Then he took a cup, and when he had given thanks, he gave it to them and they all drank from it. "This is my blood of the covenant, which is poured out for many,"

This is part of the new mysteries. It is not just for the elite. The new mysteries are for everyone. No longer can a select few prevent you from seeking mystery wisdom. All that prevents you from seeking mystery wisdom is that you don't study or practice, and you're free not to do that. So, it's the blood of the new covenant which is poured out for many.

He said to them, "Truly I tell you, I will not drink again from the fruit of the vine until that day when I drink it new in the kingdom of God."

The new blood; the new mystery.

"When they had sung a hymn they went out to the Mount of Olives. "You will all fall away," Jesus told them, "for it is written, 'I will strike the shepherd and the sheep will be scattered.' But after I have risen, I will go ahead of you.

You will all be in a spot where you forget this, forget what we're doing. You are just going to forget. That is the way it's going to happen. But after I have arisen, I will go ahead of you into Galilee because there needed to be a further teaching and that is where we were going when we talking earlier about the gnostics and all that was offered there.

Peter declared, "Even if they all fall away, I will not." "Truly I tell you," Jesus answered, "today – yes, tonight – before the rooster crows twice you yourself will disown me three times." But Peter insisted emphatically, "Even if I have to die with you, I will never disown you." And all the others said the same.

They went to a place called Gethsemane, and Jesus said to his disciples, "Sit here while I pray." He took Peter, James and John along with him, and he began to be deeply distressed and troubled. "My soul is overwhelmed with sorrow to the point of death," he said to them.

This is not sorrow for Himself, but sorrow for the condition that caused

Him to have to come back to do this. It was sorrow for everybody.

"Stay here and keep watch." Going a little farther, he fell to the ground and prayed that if possible the hour might pass from him. "Abba, Father," he said, "everything is possible for you. Take this cup from me. Yet not what I will, but what you will."

This is one of the most famous lines of this gospel. He understood that He must experience death as an innocent because the stain of the original fall was not in him. It was not there because he had the phantom within him.

Then he returned to his disciples and found them sleeping. "Simon," he said to Peter, "are you asleep? Couldn't you keep watch for one hour? Watch and pray so that you will not fall into temptation. The spirit is willing, but the flesh is weak."

This is the great drama, the dilemma, of the fall. Rudolf Steiner gives a picture of the fall within the hierarchy of the Archai, the spirits of personality. From the other hierarchies, they inherited the tendency to have a sense experience that was not simply a reflection of the creation. For the Archai, when they were having a sense experience, there was something in their realm which allowed them to have an inward experience that there was something "out there".

Prior to that, if you read Steiner's *An Outline of Esoteric Science*, on Old Saturn the experience of the hierarchies was to receive the fiat from the Father God and simply to reflect it back as a sense experience. But Rudolf Steiner gives the picture that this is called the seed germ of the senses. In order for there to be freedom, there had to be a sense body in the beings. There needed to be sensation because fiat, the creation, was separate from the created.

VI: Good Friday

For hundreds of years, the theological issue was: When God created through fiat, was God separate from the creation or included in the creation? This is a deep theological issue. This led to the schism of the western and eastern rites in Christianity over the question of an image. This is what is happening today in the Middle East with the fundamentalist Islamists trashing statues in museums. It is called an iconoclastic controversy.

The issue is the original experience that the Archai had, namely that there is an experience "out there". But the fundamentalists say, "That is not true because it is not what I and my homies believe. You had better believe it too, otherwise we are going to trash everything around you so that you don't have anything to refer to because we want to establish a new caliphate." It is predicted when that new caliphate comes, it will be the beginning of Armageddon. The fundamentalists want to be part of that because they will be among the 144,000 who will be saved. This is what is driving them, but they can't achieve that unless they have a caliphate according to the law.

We still have this issue of the falling of the sense experience into matter that gives me the experience of being separate from the creation. When I am separate from the creation, it brings about a deep anxiety. We could call it an existential anxiety, "I exist, therefore I am anxious." This dilemma is what happens in sensation.

In the original creation, there was to be a body of sensation but the purpose of it was to reflect the deed of the Creator. Thrones, Kyriotetes, Dynameis, Exousiai; they reflected the deed of the Creator. But each time it is handed down, there was a little bit of a surcharge on the sensation, until it gets to the Archai. The

Exousiai are the spirits of form. When they handed it to the Archai, they had the experience that when you have a sensation, you are going to experience form. And when they fell, the Archai had the experience that the form was "not them".

The original form was the activity of the forming; the psychic activity of the forming. The Archai was a residue of the psychic activity of the forming. There was something left over, out of their experience, which allowed them to ask, "Who is the one who is seeing what is 'out there'." That is the seed of the eventual I-being separating from the creation as individuality – freedom. But that individuality has a price, and the price is the anxiety of my freedom.

That then was passed on to the Archangels. Rudolf Steiner has a beautiful segue here, that the Archangels received the "fallen-ness" of the Archai. Not all of the Archai fell, the progressive ones are still the agents of the ability of the personality to recognize the I-being: the ability of the soul to recognize the principle of the I.

In the soul, that is what Rudolf Steiner calls "consciousness soul". The Archai are in control of that, as they are also the spirits of time. They make it possible during this time for large masses of people to begin to experience their individuality. Just look at the newspapers, it's everywhere. Spiritually, the Archai are active in this age in promoting events like the Arab Spring. Or in the great tradition of the Dalai Lama, for him to say, "I'm not going to do that anymore." That would have been unheard of 200 years ago, but it is a symptom. As Steiner said, we don't have to wait for the apocalypse. We are in it. It has already happened. We are post-apocalyptic.

So on Good Friday, there is the culmination of a weaving of these problems of separation and connection. There are many legends

VI: Good Friday

around this, and I'd like to mention one of them to give you a flavor of how this has happened. There are all of these legends around the tree of the true cross, legends of what the cross was and what it had to represent.

One of them is that Adam had Cain and Abel, and Cain killed Abel. When that happened there was a third son born, who was Seth. Adam lived to be very old and when Adam died, he had to be buried, and the people wanted to give him what in the Catholic Church is called "extreme unction". But they did not have the appropriate anointing oil, called the oil of mercy, because the oil of mercy was still in heaven.

This happened at a time when everything was "red in fang and claw", the time of "an eye for an eye and a tooth for a tooth". Not mercy but vengeance: you did this so you lose your head. So Seth, the third son, had to travel into Paradise and go to the tree guarded by the Angel with a flaming sword. He had to deal with that Angel to get the oil of mercy from the fruit of the tree of the knowledge of good and evil. But the tree of the knowledge of good and evil, and the tree of life were from one trunk that was split. And the Angel had said, "OK, Adam and Eve, you did the deed. You have access now to the tree of knowledge, but you do not have access to the tree of life because you will be called late and slow, so I am going to put a flaming sword here so that you cannot get past me to the tree of life."

Now Seth had to go back to this cherub and negotiate, because Adam had died. Seth said, "I just want some fruit from the tree of life so that I can make an anointing oil for my father, Adam, who died." The cherub allowed him to pick a fruit from the tree of life and take it back. In the fruit was a seed. Seth made anointing oil, the oil of mercy, for Adam and anointed him with it. And he took the seed from the fruit of the tree of life and put it in Adam's mouth and buried him. So out of Adam's skull came the tree of life.

The story goes that when Solomon wanted to build his temple, David had an image of the temple but he couldn't build it. Then came Hiram and the Masonic methods and stories from "the temple legend", as Rudolf Steiner called it. When they wanted to build the temple for the doorway of the holy of holies, they found this tree and cut it down. They made the timbers for the door of the holy of holies out of the tree that grew out of the skull of Adam. That is the legend.

In order to go into the holy of holies, the only one who could go in there was the priest. At a certain time in Solomon's temple, the temple of wisdom, the priest had to pass through this tree that grew out of the skull of Adam. That was where the timbers made the door of the holy of holies. Then that was lost.

Time went on until it came time for Golgotha, time for the crucifixion. When they looked around for pieces of wood, they found the timbers from that door and made the cross out of the timbers of the tree that had grown out of Adam's skull. Then they took that, and when they made the hole on Golgotha, they put the timbers of the cross in the hole. What they didn't know was that the hill of Golgotha was where Adam was buried to begin with. They put the cross on the top of Adam's skull, because Golgotha means the place of the skull.

When Christ died and they pierced his side, the blood of the covenant flowed across Adam's skull and completed a huge cosmic circuit. It completed the old mysteries, and then brought the new mysteries that were not based on blood. In the old days the power was transmitted through bloodlines. Just read the Old Testament, it is about keeping the bloodline pure.

The covenant of the new blood is for everybody, because Adam had been healed by the shedding of the blood of the new covenant of the Lamb. That is the language that they used. And then the blood that came down was gathered by Joseph of Arimathea and Nicodemus. Nicodemus was a head of the Pharisees who had a couple of secret meetings with Christ where he had a turning in his soul to the new. So he helped Joseph of Arimathea gather the blood of Christ, and together with Mary Magdalene, Joseph of Arimathea went out of the Holy Land, and started the grail stream of the feminine mysteries with the holy blood.

The mysteries of the ancient traditions were that you had to be born into the mysteries through a bloodline. And the new mysteries are the shedding of the new blood, meaning that it is not based on blood any more. It is not based on pure transmission but it is based on the fact that you, as a human, are an image of the Christ. Why? Because you are an individual, and you have within you the seed of the Son of Man. You have the potential to go to another level in your inner life where you can purify your soul to the point where it then becomes the imitation of the Christ.

Alchemically, we could ask, what is all this? It is an interesting story, but does it ring true with anything?

In my research, I try to work with embryology and physiology to understand Rudolf Steiner. I've always had an interest in biology and physiology. What I have come to understand is that the tree of life is in everybody. It is called your circulatory system. Your blood, your vascular system, is the tree of life. So what then is the tree of knowledge of good and evil? That is your nervous system. It is another tree and they are entwined with each other. One causes death and the other brings life.

Every gland that you have in your body has a nervous function, and an endocrine or a vascular function. All of your glands are fruits in your nervous system of the way your life body and your soul interact through sensation. The glands form in your physiology where sensation creates a kind of focal point.

In your inner life, your physiology is a picture of these two trees in heaven. We can ask, "Where is the cherub with the swords pointing so that we can't get access to the tree of life?" My understanding is that the cherub is represented in your pineal gland. "What is the oil of mercy?" Melatonin, because it gives mercy from this relentless sensation.

When I wake up, then I'm open to endless sensation. Every time I have a sensation in my nervous system, it triggers the vascular part of whatever gland is relevant, and creates a secretion that is an analog to the degree of the quality of the sensation. We call them neurotransmitters. Each neurotransmitter is an exact balancing and replication of the quality of the sensation. You have within you, a subtle body filled with images, energetic patterns of the becoming of your sensation. We call it endocrinology. It is a kind of "ghost" of energy in particular patterns and cadences and forms. And those energies are neurotransmitters. The neurotransmitters create our codified behaviors: wake up, freak out, procreate, lactate, migrate.

Hormonal secretions are images of the sense world but when we have our sensations, because of the fall, we have lost the experience that behind the sensation are the actions of the hierarchies. And because we've inherited from the Archai, the predilection to interpret what is out there in the sense world as separate from me, we have a tendency to be insular in our thinking. My hormones are my hormones. My response to that particular color is my response. Do you like ice-cream or not? We build repertoires of stimulus responses based on these neurotransmitters and we call it my personality. These are actually images from the cosmos, from the creative hierarchies acting in us, that we have taken and attached ourselves to.

If it were just up to the Archai and the fall, we would just be little robots. There would be a stimulus and a response and that is all. We would have the consciousness of a planarian or a sea urchin, "Oh, it's the full Moon. It's procreation time." When that's where the Moon is, then that's what happens. But we have transcended that consciousness in our humanity because in Steiner's picture, what happened when the Archangels inherited the fall from the Archai, they were given a gift from the Seraphim. The Seraphim gave to the Archangels the ability to witness the arising of the inner picture in response to the sensation. And the quality that the Seraphim gave to the Archangels to do that, is the gift of love. According to Rudolf Steiner, they were at a stage where they did not have to do this because they had already transcended the need to go through all of this human level experience. They had already gone through the human drama but they took compassion on the fact that this was eventually going to lead into a very dire strait. So they allowed the Archangels to have the experience so that they could be awake to the fact that they were separate, when they experienced this state. We call it forming a thought. And then the

Archangels passed that on to the Angels. And the Angels asked, "What do we do with this?"

Rudolf Steiner gives the picture that the Cherubim gave to the Angels the ability to interact with the inner picture, which is metanoia: I can change my inner picture. Then the Angels passed that on to us. And by the time it got to us, the creation had become really dire because we were given the pearl of great price, the ability to interact with my inner picture and the only ones who don't know that are us. So we sell that for a pot of lentils. We give it to Ahriman and Lucifer big time, all of the time.

This is then the drama of sensation. We can interact with the inner pictures that result in me from a sense experience. This is the pearl of great price in the cosmos. No other hierarchy has it. The Angels could interact with it, but they didn't have the physical environment to give them such a pronounced experience of "being separate" because their sense of interacting with it was still in the spiritual realm. Their sense had not been taken over by Lucifer until, according to Rudolf Steiner, the Old Moon period.

What I am describing to you is Old Saturn, Old Sun, Old Moon and finally we get to Earth. And Lucifer has made it so that we have the abiding experience that the blackboard over there is completely separate from me. I can touch it, I can smell it, I can taste it.

Through my sensing, I kill the world, until I awaken to the fact that in my sensing I am killing the world, and then I can change the way I respond to sensing, by trying to see the action of the hierarchies in the way the world is created. When I do that, I am participating in the development of the Son of Man. And that is what Christ came back to teach us how to do.

VI: Good Friday

To surrender to that, I have to resurrect a corpse. How do I resurrect a corpse? I have to learn about the world. I can ask myself questions like: how is aluminum made? That's why we have the capacity to learn about the world, because that learning and that thinking is the forming of a new organ of perception for the spiritual world. That is the basis of the new mysteries. That is why the book, "The Philosophy of Freedom", was important to Steiner. It's about the redemption of thinking, changing it from abstract thinking to living, pictorial thinking where I take the corpses of the world and re-animate them in myself, in order that I can experience their becoming.

When I begin to have a perception of the becoming of something, it is no longer put to death by my sense experience. I awaken in it and with it. This is the resurrection of the corpse of the world, because when I perceive the world just as a corpse, the hierarchies that are behind it are pushed out of the picture, and what enters is dogma, or corpses of the memory of what it was. Then you get organized repression.

Now we're getting to the mystery of Christian Rosenkreutz. He was invited to the wedding of the bridegroom and the bride. That's the wedding between Christ and the soul. When I marry my soul to the bridegroom, I have to experience in my soul an action of my I-being. This I-being action is to experience metanoia, to change what I think about the sense world. This is elemental perception, biodynamics and the medical work, Waldorf education, transformation of the arts and of religion, and all that Steiner labored to bring into existence. He revivified the corpses of belief structures to get back an experience of the becoming of these things in order to transform them.

So the deed of Christ on Golgotha was to become a human, in order to experience the fear that humans have about giving everything away in death. The anxiety of suffering in death is a part of the fall. To redeem that fall, by allowing the soul to say, "Even though my body passes away, I don't pass away." This is Steiner's teaching of reincarnation and the work with the dead, and all of that imaginative work to try to revivify the mystery wisdom that there is a parallel world. I always say that you have a parallel biography that you live which depends on your ability to transcend your fear of memories of sense experiences.

Alzheimer's and those kinds of disorders, even autism, being closed in, all of these things that are arising are plays of the forces that are operating in this mystery school. It's not just random. It's the new mysteries, trying to awaken people to the fact that even though a person appears to be locked in, there is a lot going on there. They are just experimenting with what it would be like to be dead.

In the movie "Awakening", based on a book by Oliver Sacks, people who are catatonic are getting L-dopa, a precursor to dopamine, and awakening to find out that they were still participating even though they were catatonic, sitting in a chair not saying or doing anything, their soul was moving along. They had a kind of disease, a sleeping sickness, that shut them out, but their soul was still active. When they took the L-dopa and started to come out of it, they rapidly progressed, because there was a part of them that had still been tracking this.

When Steiner talks about Caspar Hauser, he is speaking about the future of humanity. He is speaking about the mystery of what it will be when we awaken to the fact that sensation is killing the world.

Golgotha, the place of the skull, is a place where the cosmic drama is enacted so that the Christ being comes back in a physical body and, as it says in the gospel, "gives up the ghost". That "giving up the ghost" is a key. In Steiner's work, the phantom is one of the deepest mysteries, and as I have said, for years, I talked to people trying to find out what that is, and they would say, "Ah, well, you'll get it." It took about forty years to get the phantom, and it was still only a little piece of something huge. The picture has to do with sensation.

When you have a sense experience and your glands light off, the electrolytes in your blood are following a sequence of metals. They are exchanging energies with each other and as they exchange energies, we call it a nerve impulse, or nutrition, your cells are interacting with your blood through those metals. This is the alchemy of metals.

The pathways through which metals operate in the fluid in your body are part of the giving world of the original creation. But how you respond to them, and how you organize them is unique to your own situation. In autism, for instance, there is something called comorbidity. Comorbidity means that they cannot tell what your issues are because the lesions you have that were created by the misfiring of those neurotransmitters, create lesions in your neurology that don't allow you to get access to particular parts of your neurology. That is specific to your development. That is why autism is a spectrum of disorders rather than a specific one. Many of the things that are arising today as dysfunctions, such as multiple sclerosis, Parkinson's disease, Alzheimer's, and ALS (amyotrophic lateral sclerosis) have to do with this issue of neurotransmitters and lesions and their effect on sensation. That is the great drama of the cosmos being played out in individual lives today.

So many of the afflictions today have to do with this because it has to do with the soul interacting with the sense world in particular ways that are unique to that individual. And it's all about metanoia. And it is all a recapitulation of the crucifixion of Good Friday. And that is our inheritance, so to speak. Can I be awakened to that level in my own inner life of how sensing is creating in me memory patterns that I have access to, that are specific to the pathologies that I am experiencing in my life?

These then are the new mysteries. They involve thinking, and bringing my thinking that has no thought, into contact with sensation that has no object of sensation other than its own activity. We call it meditation.

I free my sensation from object consciousness and turn my sense experience on my own cognition whose object is sense-free. And I get exponential synergy of energy from my I-being to understand the karma of why I have these particular issues in my life. In that moment of recapitulating Good Friday, the Christ comes and says, "I can help you with this. I know what it's like, I have been there."

In order to do that, I have to train myself to focus on sense experiences where I bring my ability to witness my sense experience, and control the inner picture myself. I have to connect that ability to control the inner picture to the work of the hierarchies that are creating the world, especially the processes that the hierarchies use to create the world, like distillation or combustion. When I form symbols, images or glyphs of them and meditate on them, I'm in effect saying to the hierarchies, "Can you help me understand how this is working in my own life? I've got this thing I'm trying to work on, and I don't get it. Can you help me?"

So you find a picture in the world that reminds you of the feelings you have around the issue you're working on. It becomes a symbol for you, a metaphor of how you gain access back to the tree of life. You give the pictures that the heart is using to create the world back to them, and ask them, "Is it like this?"

And if you do that, the Christ comes in and says, "I know how that is. Here, I'll take it." And then you have a dream, or something that awakens you to the potentials of things, or at least the holiness of your suffering, which is better than being really upset about it. Because if I'm really angry about my suffering, it's doubled.

So, find a symbol and hold it, and find how the symbol becomes that thing, whatever it is. If it's a kind of plant, picture how the plant grows. Don't just picture the plant as a snapshot because if you picture the plant as a snapshot, it's just a corpse. And your consciousness will be corpse-like because it's just a snapshot of a thing. But if you picture the plant growing for example, your consciousness pulls your soul away from Lucifer and Ahriman, and says, "Excuse me, but I am involved in a dialogue with the hierarchies that stand behind the becoming of this sense experience. So guess what, you're not invited to the party."

So that's what I have been given from the dilemma of the Archangels and the Angels. I have been given that tool. The Christ had to come down to meet the Pistis. And what Mary his mother tells him is the imagination she had when the Angel Gabriel came and told her she was going to be the mother of God. She shares that with Christ. She is the only one who could do that. It is just such an amazing image of what she felt when she heard the news that He was coming. She tells Him about that. Even He couldn't know that, but she could because she is a human. This is a big deal, and it is up to humans.

The resurrection is up to humans. It has been accomplished and there is a seed in you. That is a done deal. But now we have to search for the new Isis, by using what have been given to us as capacities by the hierarchies that are latent in our own physiology. They are embedded in our physiology, but they have been overcome by the adversaries. We need to take them back from the adversaries, by saying, "I'm going to work on this myself." It has to do with sensations and neurotransmitters and all of that stuff, but they are just the corpus of the energy involved in sense activity and forming of memory.

Memory is a big issue today. Ahriman wants it big time. He wants memory because he understands that if humans have memory, he doesn't get access to it. If humans claim their own memory, then their memory is not on the menu of what he can access, and there is no app to facilitate it. You are the app.

Holy Week and Golgotha is not something that happened in the past—it is happening all the time. Now, as we are here in the world, it is the continual unfolding of this new mystery school that was inaugurated by Christ. And then all of the teachers have come back and said, "You need to do this so that this will happen." That has become a dogma, but it is my experience that Rudolf Steiner cut right through and pierced the veil, so to speak, by saying, "It's about freedom."

Glyph for Saturday — Purification

Purification (2 variations)

So, taking into sleep these two glyphs of purification. You saw this in the alchemical manuscript. I talked earlier about dealbation: the purifying of the salt. First you purify the oil, then you purify the alcohol. If you keep distilling alcohol, it becomes so fine it gets to be what we call ether. Ether is alcohol, but highly, highly distilled, highly refined, highly purified. The higher we get in purification, the closer our consciousness comes to be able to say, "Yes, I think this area in Sector C is problematic."

Purification is the glyph and you can take either one.

Description of the movement of glyph: I start up somewhere and then I follow matter, then matter comes down and gets clogged, and then matter goes down and gets clogged, and then I do something with it and distill it and it goes up into a higher state. The repetition of falling down and lifting up is a metaphor for the inner life. Christian Rosenkreutz taught that the best way to do that is to bring the glyphs into sleep and then retrieve them in the morning. Taking a glyph like this into sleep begins to change how your REM state happens, and your REM state is where all of the neurotransmissions are happening.

An audience member asks, What happens if you wake up at four in the morning?

That is great because that means you are online. The reason you wake up at 4 AM is because the Earth is breathing out where you are, and your soul is breathing out with it. The Angels know that a 4 AM call is the best. That is the way they do it. Spend a little time, 10 or 15 minutes, trying to be silent. Then go back to sleep again.

You will have excellent dreams. They're not always about butterflies but what happens is that you're awakening in a spot where you're normally asleep and that's where we're going to go tomorrow. Have good dreams.

HOLY SATURDAY

We could put a subtitle to this, "The Transformation of the Senses". In my understanding, that is the central issue in the Rosicrucian work. In this idea in Holy Week, the new mysteries are based on the transformation of the senses. The old mysteries were based on getting in line with the creation, as it was given. And the new mysteries recognize that there is a glitch in that, and it is your sensation, so you need to work on that.

The "given" in philosophy is the form of the creation as it is perceived by us. They call that science. But there's a problem in that, because we have lost sight of the fact that behind the creation there is divinity. Science has said that it is a kind of subjective thing, so if you come here looking for theology, you're in the wrong building. But in the ancient world, theology and science were the same thing. They had to separate because theology became so fragmented by everybody's belief structure through their fundamentalism. Today we even have scientific fundamentalism, which is climate change assertion or climate change denial. So that has to change, no matter what it is. It could be fundamentalism about this coffee being better than another one. Being vegan can be a new religion. Or the Sacramento Kings basketball team can be seen as a new religion with a new temple being built downtown.

Our senses are the source of fundamentalism in the way we experience them. They were not designed to be experienced that way. They were designed to reflect the creation with joy, but there was a problem with that, and that was that the creation is not the creator. There was a separation and in the esoteric language, a separation between two things creates a space or a lacuna. And that space is the doorway to perdition. That is, the astral body is the space between spiritual reality and my sensory experience in my body. That's called the astral realm, or the realm of the soul.

It is a hollowing out between the reality of the divine world and the manifest world, and we are embedded in it because our spirit is in matter or in flesh. Kurt Vonnegut says, "The mud gets up and talks." You know, it's a weird way to put it, but it puts its finger on the dilemma of the human, "Am I my body or am I something that's invisible? And does something invisible remain when my body goes away? Is that thing that's invisible still present or not?" And if you think that when the body goes away it's the end, then you try to get as many toys in your toy box as possible before it ends. Whether your toys are knowledge or gear or money or fame or whatever, you try to pack in as much as you can before you check out.

If you think that's the end, I come in, I am a sorry guest on this dark Earth, and then I check out — and who cares? So in contemporary life, there's a kind of existential malaise because we're put in this very weird position of coming in naked as it's said, a tabula rasa, an empty slate. And then we fill it with weird stuff and then we check out. It's senseless, it's ridiculous. Steiner says it all the time. It's a ridiculous view. Who would want to sign up for that?

So the sense organs, in the way they are configured, give us a very skewed picture of the relationship between the spiritual world and the manifest world that started on Old Saturn. Through the fall of the spirits of darkness, the Archai awakened to the fact that their sensing was giving them an impression of something that was not them. We could say "other", a radical other, no matter what that is, but it was still in a spiritual condition. So it could be remedied by gifts of love and harmony from the hierarchies. And that is a beautiful picture of the doorway through which the Christ came because it was understood, in what Rudolf Steiner called the lodge of the great beings who are serving all of this, that there was going to be a problem eventually. The creation was going to fall so deeply into a course, that the beings who would be caught in that experience would have no recourse except to succumb to the illusion of being separate from the creation.

They would just have to abide by that because there was nothing in the system that could counter that because the creation didn't include that, and it couldn't include that because that is freedom. It's a great dilemma.

So the ancient people said, "Don't even get involved in it. It's not going to end well." That was before Golgotha. Don't bother. Just go back into heaven where all of God's children have a place in the choir. Just pick up your sheet music and sing along. And the laws that came down from that were just to sing along. This is the Pharisees and scribes. "Just sing along and everybody can be happy."

So in the sense world, every time you have a sensation, it's a recapitulation of the fall. The way the senses are organized, all sensation is again, the fall, unless we become conscious of how the sensation is impacting us.

And then this is called marriage and family counseling. What happens when dad comes home and just says, "This is what is happening." You need to change that and you need to become aware. And Dad needs to become aware of the problem when he comes home and says this is what's happening for everybody else. But he's probably not going to do that because he's still living by the role of: "This is my kingdom. Here's the sheet music. Sing along."

So the awakening in myself to how I am responding to sense experiences, builds an organ of perception to perceive how somebody else is experiencing what I am putting out. That is the Rosicrucian work. I have to awaken in the other, and the only way I can do that is by assimilating the corpses of my wound. This is the Ouroboros. I have to eat my own tail.

That's an alchemical principle. I have to assimilate the shadow as a wounded healer. People will be irresistibly attracted to you when you have overcome a shadow, because they will want to know how you overcame your shadow. You become what Jung called "the wounded healer". You can't be a healer unless you are wounded.

This is Saint Paul, "My strength is made perfect in my weakness." This is a difficult thing to understand, but my weakness is the scar of uncognized sense experience. We call it memory. I hear something. I see something. I taste something. I feel something. If I'm touched in the wrong way, I can form some patterning of touch that says, "When I get pressured like this, I'm in fight or flight."

The memory bank of sensation is where the shadows are, and I have to go back into them, and reopen that wound in order to heal it and then to cauterize it. This involves healing and medicines and all of that. I have to provide my body with a whole other level of sensation.

And the irony of that, and what the Rosicrucians understood, was that substance is sensation solidified. Substances are behavioral patterns. And we have affinities for them. We even name them:

theobromine, which means this substance is related to God. Theobromine is the active chemical in chocolate, which is related to God. We all know that.

So it's in our language, and the alchemist said this is just another level of language, to take substances and to try to find how this substance triggers a particular sensation. There is healing in that if we lift the substance back into a dynamic rather than a cause, this is homeopathy.

The role of sensation as something that has fallen, is the root of the new mysteries. That means I have to somehow get in contact with what happens when I have a sensation of an image, what happens in me and what feelings do I associate with that, that come out of me as a kind of projection.

This is the basis of what we're doing in the crucible exercise. So when you look at a picture and you form a question, and you bring it out, you are going through a whole inner process of purification of sense activity, because you are bringing the sense activity that is below the threshold up into consciousness. You are lifting it and your I-being gets access to that when you form a question.

That's the purpose of the crucible exercise, and that's the purpose of the crucible of Holy Week, for Christ to go so deeply into matter that He experiences death, so that He can go through it and come back on the other side cognitively. So this is what humans are freaked out about. So in Gethsemane, when He says, "I am agitated to death, I am terror stricken, please take this away." That is all the way down to the edge.

And then, "I understand this needs to happen, so it will happen if you will it." So in order for the cosmos to turn, a divine being had to experience that fear of how the body of sensation is going to be extinguished. And the question is: am I still going to exist?

So this then is the role of sensation. The key to the Rosicrucian work and the alchemical work is to learn how to use your sensations as a video rather than a snapshot. I have to frame the snapshots in a sequence in order to free them up from the corpus of my conditional belief that this is what this is.

This is present in language; it's present in music. This is why we're so deeply attracted to video because it's giving us the impression that we're actually doing the work that we're supposed to be doing. But we're not. It's kind of a placeholder.

So the forming of an image and then connecting that to another image and then connecting that to yet another image in my own freedom is the work of rectifying errors based on past memories. We call it thinking, but because we're trained the way we are, our thinking always ends up in a thought that becomes another corpse.

So the method is to give yourself pictures where you sequence them, form a question, and then if you really want to get the energy going, think the sequence of the pictures backwards, and you'll see what was there before you formed the question. Before you formed the question about the sensation, there was already a predilection for the answer, and you have to find out what that is, because that goes back to when you were one year old.

What condition triggers the sensation that I keep setting up for myself? Steiner says somebody walks down the street, a brick falls out of a building and hits them on the head and they say, "Oh, this is terrible!" But what they didn't realize was that the invisible part of them went up and pushed the brick to the edge.

VII: Holy Saturday

So they're walking and then they go into blame and shame, instead of asking, "Why did I need this?" they ask, "Why does this keep happening to me? What's the matter with you, world?" You're setting it up because of sensation. Sensation means, "That brick was up there and hit me in the head, I'm going to find a lawyer and make some money out of this."

But Steiner said you put it up there so you could experience that blow as an awakening to consciousness—if you could have the real picture of the Son of Man. But if you don't have the picture of the Son of Man, then you're looking for a lawyer or a Pharisee or a politician to solve it. But the only one who can solve it is you.

So we're going to do the crucible exercise now, and you can take anything that is there in the Tree of Life diagram.

But I'm going to form the space for the questions. You have to connect one of the sections we did before to another section, instead of asking questions about one element only. One form of question might be "I wonder why 'study' is connected to 'work'." You could use "universalem" or the little sun up there. So your questions are linking questions; they are video questions rather than snapshots.

Let's stop there. Can you feel this? When we were asking questions about each single thing, you could get an answer. But these questions are much deeper because we're exploring the field of the whole thing, rather than individual units. The work with the senses is to try to expand your field awareness through as many senses as possible.

The function of the arts is to bring consciousness to the way my body feels when it moves, the way my voice feels when it speaks, the way it feels when the color is right. Is there enough salt in the kvass? Whatever it is, the art is a kind of titration and balancing of the senses so that I can have the experience that my consciousness permeates the senses, rather than just being an unconscious river which is flowing along underneath.

So the role of the arts, even the role of science, was intended to do that at the time of the alchemists. The sense world was very much where they did their experimentation. They had an apparatus, but it was a very simple apparatus, because the meter was them. The goal of the science experiment was to harmonize one's own consciousness with what was happening. It was understood that what was happening in the substance was an analog of consciousness. Today, the analog of consciousness is placed in the technology of instrumentation. You're only as good as your instrument. So we build a Hadron Collider with 17 miles of magnets, and there's a short circuit in one, and there goes a billion dollars a day to fix the thing. This is where sensation has gone. Somehow the instrumentation is the replacement of sensation, but in the end you have to have a pair of eyeballs look at the photo plates to determine whether or not the particle is there.

Billions of dollars are being spent on these projects and it's getting crazy because of computer enhancement of images. If you actually saw the raw shots taken from the Hubble telescope it would be a big yawner, but they're all colored nicely. They blend infrared with visible red and a little touch of the ultraviolet, and gamma ray, that's our filter. It's like painting. And we look at it and say, "Wow, that's awesome." But if you were out there, you wouldn't see anything unless you were a honeybee.

So, that quality of sensation today has been even more removed from us by the reliance on instrumentation. Because of what?

VII: Holy Saturday

Because our senses are "too weak".

So, as we penetrate this on Holy Saturday, there was a drama now that Christ had died, was murdered in a body of flesh, and His blood had touched the skull of Adam, and the original covenant had been completed with the Father God.

In the alchemical tradition, there's something called the debt to the Father God. The debt to the Father God is that you must return the dust back to the Father God. So from dust you have come, and to dust you shall return. The debt to the Father God is that in the dust is a residue of what your soul has experienced while it was in the dust.

The dust is a kind of akashic bank of sensation, and that makes the soul experiences based on the sensations of a human, a turning point of the cosmos. Because how you are experiencing in your flesh what is happening in the creation is changing the creation. This is the photon slit experiment in physics. How my consciousness interacts with the photons. Is the way my consciousness interacts the way in which the world is created? Or is the created world a done deal and I'm just flying around on a barren rock? Even though it's a scientific question, it's also a theological question.

So the issue of sensation is that the creation, because of human sensation, has fallen and condensed and condensed and condensed into an ash. And all of the aspects that constitute this spiritual ontogeny, this spiritual line of emergence of a human, are condensed in patterns in that ash.

There's an ash of what the I-being will be and I call that ash of the I-being, the "great me." It's not my I-being, it's me. Me is different than I. I have the perception that my I and your I are one. Me is like,

"What are you doing in my space, in my I?"

There is a funny thing about freedom because the highest freedom is to give your freedom for somebody else. That's love. But the me says, "No, this is my space. Get out of my space or pay me something for being in it. Give me a dollar. That will be OK. Entrance fee, one dollar."

So that experience of the falling of the spiritual human, with all of the I-being and the potential for consciousness soul, and all the soul qualities, and then the physical qualities, and the matter and fluid body of endocrine patterns, and the air quality of communication; all of that condensed into what we now call Earth. Because in the spiritual condition, we were embedded in that spiritually, by being part of the creation of the hierarchies that were creating the Earth as an image of the human, as mother, which every indigenous culture recognizes. Our father as the sky and our mother as the Earth, hear us and give us peace.

So the mother, the matrix, has fallen from a spiritual condition, as humans free themselves from the fall of the sensation that was deposited as ash in the body of the Earth. That's an alchemical picture.

So in the mineral realm, if you want a picture of this, look at the summary of the nine spheres of Earth at the end of this section. There's been a great tradition of this idea of the nine spheres. In the third century, Saint John Chrysostom had an Easter homily about what happened on Holy Saturday when the earthquake came and Christ's body fell into a crack in the Earth. His physical body fell into a crack in the Earth on Good Friday at the crucifixion, where it says, "He gave up the ghost." And on Holy Saturday when he was interred in the Earth, he became the spirit of the Earth, and as they say, the Lord of the Elements.

This is a deep secret mystery from Christian Rosenkreutz that Christ is now in your retort. You think you're doing a distillation, but you're actually doing the Last Supper. The teaching of the falling led to the idea that the Earth is an image of the human, but fixed in a kind of negative way because it is a corpus of all the potential sensations that a human could create, that have led to this densification of the creation, so that there is a bunch of humans running around on the Earth thinking that they have nothing to do with the divine world. This is contemporary life. I can be as bad as I want to be. I can lie as much as I want in public, and you need to figure it out so who cares? Just give me the money.

That consciousness is the best process for the Earth. We can pretty much see it. And as that happened, it was understood that Christ on Holy Saturday went through the solidified sheaths of the human, through the Earth to the center of the Earth, bringing light to the corpus of the cosmic human, which is the body of the Earth.

You know, you used your mom's body to get here, so do we all. And the debt to the Father was that you had to give back to your mother whatever you borrowed, so that the mother could evolve along and keep pace with what was happening with humans. But in the ancient world, the mysteries evolved to the point where you didn't have to give your body back. You could take the forces of consciousness that you learned, and put them in an amulet or a talisman or a drum or some idol, and put that in Switzerland and then check out and then come back again and pick that up and do magic with it. That's the decadence of the old mysteries, because there were these holy places where there were holy things. But then there were other places where there were unholy things working against the holy things. By having these little power reservoirs: allies, amulets, traditions, and places to put the power reservoirs and power sectors, you get past the debt to the Father. You concentrate in those objects, the consciousness that needs to go back to the Earth in order that the Earth can evolve.

That is why the old mysteries became decadent and that is why Christ needed to come back and say, "You know, there are new mysteries that need to happen." But we're late and slow and I always say, "You can't turn Queen Mary in a tea cup." It takes a long time to turn this puppy around to get it back to the spot where we realize, "Oh my God, me doing something affects the Earth!"

Back in the day, you just dumped stuff in the creek, but "Hey, that's not in my backyard." Now my backyard extends pretty far out there. So that is a lifting of consciousness we could say, even in a Rosicrucian way, we become aware that we are all connected through the Earth and the forces of the Earth. Because when Christ on Holy Saturday went into the Earth, he went all the way to the very center of the Earth and did a process called "the harrowing of hell".

Harrowing means cultivating, breaking up, and making something permeable. You break up the soil to make it vulnerable, harrow it to make it possible to put in a crop. Christ had to harrow hell that was represented by the fixed nature of the layers of Earth. And the homily of John Chrysostom was about the different layers of Earth. Then Rudolf Steiner, in just three or four lectures, brought that up and put it out and then went away. A couple years ago there was a book called "*The Inner Life of the Earth*", and some of us were asked to write some essays. The harrowing of hell is then a recapitulation of Christ going through the corpses that were created in the Earth body as humans cast off minerals, and cast off actually having plants. However, we are finding that our microbiome has more DNA in it and the bacteria in the gut than is in the whole body, so we are still carrying plants around. We are still carrying minerals around. We are still carrying air around. But the big portion of that has been cast off and has become the Earth as a corpse. But now Christ has entered that through the harrowing of hell.

So here's the picture. The first layer of the Earth is the mineral earth, and that is a representative of the physical body that has become manifest as a substance. The thing that allows the physical body to become manifest as a substance is that it is perceptible to my senses. According to Rudolf Steiner, the thing that allows that to happen is that the physical body is actually an invisible body of forces that is permeated by ash. Call it ash, calcium or potassium or whatever. Potassium in your blood is an ash of the metal. Potassium as a metal is actually an activity, but as a substance, it has become a kind of ash that has precipitated out of the activity of potassium as a worldwide event.

Potassium is a worldwide event dynamically, spiritually, but as a substance, it falls out and becomes this thing in the bottom of the retort. That's the physical earth that has become a corpse because it has become matter. Its becoming is still the physical body but you can't see it. That's the physical earth that needed to be redeemed.

Then the layer below that is what is known as the liquid earth, that is the equivalent of the life body. This is where the mineral becomes sentient. This is humus. This is soil and the cationic exchange capacity in the soil, the clay. This is the exchange of solutions across membranes within the plant life, and then through the chemistry of photosynthesis, and the transformation of minerals into substances with energy and light. This is what is known as the liquid earth. Because it's earth; it's potassium, calcium, magnesium and whatever but it's liquid. If we took all of that liquid out, we would have a kind of shadow earth that was just the universal flow of potassium seeking calcium. That's the liquid earth, and it's a corpse of the spiritual relationship between the spiritual being of calcium and the spiritual being of magnesium as a metal.

The metals in the past were gods, and alchemists understood that Zeus is tin and Mars is iron. Consciousness of iron is the planet Mars, and that's a dynamic. So Christ had to go into the water earth because life as potential gets fixed in the liquid in certain patterns. This is all about patterns, and a rubric for that is something that in alchemy or in esoteric work, is called "form". Form is the process of forming, and it is not random. In chemistry, they call it elective affinity. This is a particular molecular bonding angle of water that has a relationship to carbon, and that allows the hydrogen and oxygen and the carbon to form a bond to make a scaffolding. That patterning comes from somewhere, and if you try to check that in a regular science book today, the answers about why it happens are always tautological, always circular logic. This happens because of that, but that happens because of this. No one really knows why the bonding angle of water is 104.5°. So, here's the book, just sing along with the choir. The liquid earth had to be penetrated with consciousness of the divine being.

Then the air earth is the astral air element, which in the language is called steam earth or vapor earth. It is the will-like nature of the patterning. What if there were a pattern that we could call potassium? Potassium is "potash", which is what happens when you burn a stick, you get ash. You put the ash in water; you extract the water; you boil the water off, and what you are left with is potassium carbonate or potash. So the word potash is actually a picture of a dynamic, a process, a burning and a reconstituting. So the air element is the will where that imagination of that substance could become that thing; the will to become potassium. That had to be penetrated; that's the air earth.

Then the next level is the form earth. It's sometimes called the soul earth or the fire earth because this form is the potential for a will impulse to give rise to a substance. We could call it an idea. The idea that a will impulse could eventually become potassium, and have something to do with the way in which growth would happen: that is a part of the Earth. It's beyond the will; it's in the realm of ideas. This kind of thinking goes back through John Chrysostom in the fourth century, then through the Chartres masters in the way they describe how chemistry was happening through the alchemists in the 1400s. Then it died a strange death in the 1600s in the Enlightenment, but it was present, still underground, in the Rosicrucian work in the 16th and 17th centuries. Then the idea was resurrected by Goethe in German idealism. And it eventually came to us as the stream of understanding that behind substance are beings willing and having ideas, that became then a corpse, because of the direction that the cosmos was going, in order that humans could have the sense experience that they were separate from everything.

The need to do that is the basis of our sense of freedom that needs to be redeemed. The form earth is like a negative cast. If you want to make a sculpture, you make a sculpture. But if you want to replicate that sculpture, if you want to have it happen again and again and again, you make what an artist would call a form. So with the first sculpture you make, you form that form and then you put that in a plaster form, and then you take the plaster form that's a negative of the form that you have formed, and then you pull the form off, and you have a final form.

That's our language.

So that gives a picture of the dilemma of form. When we say form, what do we mean by that? We mean everything from the idea to the actual thing to a replication of it; an image of it. So this form earth is the place where that replication of the potential for capacity happens. That's a repository of the "negative forms that will resolve in forms that become form". It's difficult languaging, but that's because English is so poetic. There are multiple meanings for everything. So that's the form earth.

With those four, the mineral earth, the liquid, the air, and the form earth, Christ went down and redeemed the four elements, which is what we all have in our bodies. But then going in deeper, we get not just the elements, but we start to move into the congealed soul activities. So the next in sequence is what Rudolf Steiner called the "fruit earth". The fruit earth consists of expansive growth at the expense of consciousness.

This is a hard thing to understand, but your consciousness as a human being extinguishes your life. It uses it up. This is called nutrition, assimilation and excretion. The degree of consciousness that you bring and the quality of the food that you eat lifts consciousness, so that you become kind of destructive of the physical world as you move up in consciousness. This is why some people can get so high in consciousness, they don't actually have

VII: Holy Saturday

to eat anymore. They live in another dimension of substance. Now we're getting to the mysteries of the soul. In the fruit earth, there is this great potential for understanding how consciousness diminishes life and makes a corpse out of life. As Steiner says, there are potential burgeoning, teeming energies that are the archetypal source of all life. All life arises from these teeming chaotic energies, which are in your gastrointestinal tract, which is a jungle of stuff happening. There is a lot of work being done now because it alters your consciousness, the population in your jungle. It has a lot to do with who you think you are and who you think is the one that is involved with theobromine in chocolate.

Your gut flora have a big input into the way in which the sensations around your digestion respond. I once had to do a candida fast for a year because of an overgrowth of yeast due to all kinds of stuff that happened in my youth. And I was on this fast for about a year and then I was going through Raley's grocery store one day and I saw bouillon cubes and something in me went, "Oh!" I went home and put a bouillon cube in water, and it was so good. Then I was talking in class and I mentioned that I'd been really suffering on this fast for the past year, but bouillon cubes were solving it for me and they were really great. Then someone very discreetly came up after class and said, "You know what's in the bouillon cube? It's yeast."

So my yeast was dying and saying, "I need some yeast. Go eat yeast!" My jungle was saying to go over and get that because we need it. We need reinforcements. So that's the fruit Earth: burgeoning forces. Rudolf Steiner said this is the source of volcanoes in the Earth. It's just out of control. Just eat! Eat! I'm going to eat Hawaii.

Then the next one down is the fire earth. Where up above there was will in the air earth, this fire earth down below is pure passion for just "having my way". And that is a layer in the Earth. Steiner calls it the passion layer that drives the life of sensation: the drive to get another sensation. You can't eat just one sensation. I guess we could call it the potato chip level of the Earth. Or the peanut level.

Steiner says this consists of drives and instincts for pleasure and gratification. It is actually a level in the Earth that has become solidified that is the source of catastrophic forces that rise up and just go rampant, such as weather phenomena and hurricanes. They rise up and consume through the life of sensation.

Now we're down in the soul room. It's my experience that these types of phenomena are triggered by relationships, angular relationships between planets. I just found a quote in one of Steiner's books about Kepler. Kepler says, "If you really want to understand the soul of the Earth," which is where we are now, we're down in the solidified earth salt, "you will not understand the soul of the Earth unless you pay attention to how the weather responds to planetary aspects." That's Kepler's *Harmonices mundi, book five*.

So in that realm, when we get down here, the soul of the Earth has received a kind of exudate from humans trying to free themselves, and become this dark force that arises. It's the chaos force in the natural world. Sometimes, especially here on the West Coast, in tree-hugger world, nature is thought of as all benign. But it's not all benign, just look at Fukushima.

So we as humans look at those kinds of cascades and say, "It's evil." But it's not evil. It is just dark and it needs to be penetrated because it's an aspect of our own sense life in our own soul. It is a passion for just more and more sensation, which is OK but we need to understand when it's happening, that this is what's happening

VII: Holy Saturday

in me. I need to understand that my consciousness in Raley's grocery store was not my consciousness, it was the consciousness of my flora. And that's not even bad because candida is 40% of the inflammation that takes over once you take a good hit of a broad spectrum antibiotic. You kill everything except the candida, because the candida has been given to you to keep you in business. But unfortunately the candida is voracious and eats all the other beneficial flora when they try to repopulate again. And people are saying this is a source of all kinds of disease processes and autoimmune responses today. So the immune system triggers on the proteins that are created by the candida. That's how the T-cells recognize, "I should kill this," or "No, I should save this because this is actually part of the organism I'm trying to save". Passion.

Science is finding these things, but if you said, "Oh, that's part of the fire earth." They would ask, "What are you talking about?" It's just a different way of understanding what is happening in the world today.

Next level is the earth reflector. This is where the form that is contained at one level as a form, is turned inside out and becomes its opposite. Everything that is formed is programmed to go to its opposite. This is just a law of nature. For everything that is going in one direction, there's a part of the Earth that says, "No, I think you're actually going to go in the opposite direction." I don't know about your life, but you decide you want to go over here but you end up over there. That's a counter image of the form principle of the first action that has been solidified into the Earth as the earth reflector.

It's a quality of the Earth that the Earth carries and it says, "Here's a process going and it's going to go so far that it's going to flip to its opposite." In consciousness, that's catharsis. It goes so far in one direction that you flip to the opposite and that gives you catharsis. You could call it healing, but there's always a crisis, known as the healing crisis. The system has to go to chaos in order to reverse. That's the reflector. The opposite has to happen.

In the next layer, the earth fragmenter, all life is fragmented. As we get deeper into the Earth, there is this exudate of the fall that gets so dense that it has to vaporize and annihilate everything and go to the periphery. If that didn't happen, there would be no future. If you didn't annihilate your sandwich, you would have a headache, because you need to annihilate that food in order that the wisdom of your organism can rebuild it back up, in your own image. So you have in you a fragmenter that sends your sandwich into a whole other place, and if it doesn't, then you have something called leaky gut syndrome.

So the Earth has one of those layers of the fragmenter, but in the fragmenter everything gets reversed, including good intentions and moral initiatives.

With the fragmenter earth, we get down into the soul of the earth that has taken the hit for this rejection or this casting off of these forces. These forces of chaos and darkness and catastrophe and annihilation become social and moral problems for us.

And Christ in the wisdom of being a member of the Trinity, had to come into the Earth and say, "For all you beings in this part of the Earth, there is new news. You'll still be in business, but the people up there will be able to redeem you because I'm going to put a seed here of the potential for them to realize that it's their own sensation that is keeping the earthquakes happening." Hence Steiner's famous quote, "it's human consciousness that creates

VII: Holy Saturday

the weather". Because human consciousness is unconscious about planetary aspects they just amplify these things through the Earth. And then we get Hurricane Katrina.

There are laws around this and we have to talk to Pythagoras about how this works, but the Earth responds to that, because those parts of the shadow of Earth are remnants of what used to be human consciousness that was fixed into the Earth as a kind of corpus, and that had to be redeemed. And that's then the harrowing of hell.

Then finally, the earth core is the source of immoral forces. All of this prior stuff is amoral. It can still be nasty, but it's amoral. But the core earth is immoral. It is discord and separation and hate. And the kicker here is that the forces of the earth core are used by black magicians. Here we get to the old mysteries and the new mysteries, because black magicians used hate as the ultimate tool because hate is the absolute opposite of love.

And the forces of the dark core of the earth can be used in such a way that they can be amplified and then projected. Then we get to Ahriman and devices and the morality of devices basically. We're free to create all kinds of stuff but it's like the sorcerer's apprentice. You can start a lot of stuff. "Can you stop it? Can you store nuclear waste products? Oh, we can make them. Sure, but can you store them? With their half-life of a billion years or more? Yeah. We'll put it in this crack over here. It's all right, somebody else will have to worry about it."

This core earth becomes really critical today because of the need for transforming the immoral use of power.

Christ on Holy Saturday went all the way down into the realm of black magicians at the core and planted a seed for the eventual potential for the Earth to become a new Sun. In order for the Earth to become a new Sun, all matter has to be brought back into its state of form, its activity, through imaginative consciousness having to do with humans redeeming their sense-life. When that happens, Steiner said there are whole technologies available to us that will work on moral forces of the human. Then there are technologies available that will work on the immoral forces of a human but they always use the life of the human as the force. There is all kinds of stuff written about that, such as by John Keely and the Keely motor. Keely died of Crohn's disease. Crohn's disease is like ulcerative colitis. He basically used up his digestive apparatus in the devices.

In the beginning, that didn't happen to him because he wasn't involved in money. He was just creating. But as he got devices, the robber barons bank-rolled him, and he started having visions of more and more precious metals to make the devices. They wanted a device that would bore a hole in the mountain to get gold. They wanted a device to make a flying saucer that would be able to transport the gold. So they bankrolled him and he kept building the devices. But they wanted the devices to be made so that anybody could work them. Unfortunately, the only one who could work them was Keely. As the devices got finer and finer, his morality for doing it became shabbier and shabbier. It became involved just in money, and the devices used him rather than allowing for that to happen. This is Franklin's time, but in Hebrew, it's the Gollum: the device that I create then eats me.

In our future, there will be devices that may be made that run on moral forces because Christ harrowed hell on Holy Saturday. The question is, can I transform my senses to the degree that I can tell what is moral and what is not?

Summary of the nine spheres of earth

1. Mineral earth – physical body (earth element) solid rock

2. Liquid earth – etheric body (water element) rock milk has the quality of sentience/sensitive (plant like) except that it is the exact opposite to life. Life dies in this layer. This layer is explored by pure concentration by an occultist.

3. Air earth – astral body (air element) steam earth, vapor earth, full of life, will-like nature. Great expansive powers. Inverted consciousness/inverted feelings. This layer destroys or extinguishes sensations by turning them into the opposite.

4. Form earth – soul earth potential for substances to arise, once more a recapitulation of the physical or mineral but in potential – pure astrality – negative form of all things manifest at the mineral layer – like a template that is continually producing manifest forms but its form is in the negative. All of the qualities of an object pass out into its surroundings; the actual space of the object being emptied.

5. Fruit earth – the earth of expansive growth, primal source of all lower life (transformed life forces in thinking process relates this level to mind soul) (warmth ether) living matter/no corpus/pure potential, burgeoning , teeming energies that are the archetypal source of all life. All life arises from this. Volcanic forces relate this layer to the fire earth – forms arising and disappearing. This layer is the underlying life that serves the layers above it. Related to thinking and mental image.

6. Fire earth – pure will and feelings. Passion layer – composed entirely of passions (sensations). When the sensations are transformed this layer relates to consciousness soul. (Light ether). Drives, instincts, sentience of pleasure and pain amplified into catastrophic forces. Volcanic forces relate this layer to the fruit earth. Intimately linked to human will, this layer consists entirely of passions.

7. Earth Reflector – (tone ether) inner morality (immorality) of natural forces. Like a prism that dissolves everything reflected in it and manifests the counter image.

8. Fragmenter – number generator, living forms generated many times over, unrest, disharmony and immorality. All life is fragmented and reduced to infinity. This layer shatters moral qualities and multiplies the immoral ones. Raying up through the earth, this force brings disharmony and evil into the world.

9. Earth core – source of immoral forces, discord, separation and hate used by black magicians.

Glyph for Sunday – Sublimation

Sublimation

EASTER SUNDAY

The image above is an alchemical diagram of the relationship between what's known as salt and sulfur. This relates to the idea of form and then sublimation. The alchemist had a word for the way in which the invisible became visible. They would look at the phenomenon of a salt crystal coming out of the solution of salt. A solution is invisible and the crystal itself is visible. This movement from the invisible to the visible is called "salt", or sometimes "sal" – a sal process. The process of coming from the invisible to the visible creates the substance "sal". But the process "sal" is going from the precipitate back into the invisible, because the substance is weaving and going back into its dynamic. Substances are only active in the body when they are being destroyed. That's life. So if your calcium isn't mobile then you have deposits. What makes it mobile is your I-being, being active in the will to create fire, to keep the levity force in your blood so that the calcium stays up. The nitrogen in your blood needs to be activated by your will force, or it forms crystals and falls down to your feet and then you have gout.

The I-being represents a force of levity that lifts substance up into a dynamic. When that dynamic weakens, the substance falls back out as a manifestation, as a corpse; that's called sal. In the diagram there, you see that when sal has substance, the arrows are going out. That little dot in the center could be a cube of salt that you put in water and then it goes out and becomes invisible. That's the upper part of the diagram.

In the lower part of the diagram, the arrows are coming in. The sal process is precipitation, but the substance goes back out again. The substance has a yearning to become imponderable, but the imponderable has a yearning to become ponderable. This is sal.

So when you go to sleep, you are imponderable and you have a yearning to become ponderable. You call it waking up in the morning.

Your senses are a sal substance, because you look out and say, "That's a tree out there." That's sal. But if you see the tree inwardly as a becoming, you're lifting the corpse of the memory into a process, and we call that imagination. The problem with imagination is that it's personal to you based on the memories that form the imagination to begin with. You have to be able to check your memory and see, is this thing I'm remembering actually tallying up with something other than my spleen? Is this real? Is it doing what I'm saying it's doing? And that process is that you have to learn that the gravity/levity pole in the self has another component, and that's the energetic component that allows the substance to go into solution. When the substance goes into solution that is more what they call sulf or sulfur, that's more of a combustion process. It's going out of manifestation into a realm of potential.

In plants, that's the forming of oils, especially essential oils that evaporate and go to the periphery if you leave the cap of the bottle off. So sulfur also, if you look at the diagram there, sulfur goes out. But the arrows in the upper part where it says sulfur as a substance, the arrows are going out and in at the same time because sulfur is a rock that you can light on fire with a match. When the people saw that, it was like, "Whoa!"

And there are special properties from that rock. You can find sulfur in the hot springs of California where the sulfur water comes out, that's hot from the flume and it meets the cold water. It looks like egg yolk around the rock. That sulfur is a kind of a liquid rock that when it goes into a sal condition of cold becomes congealed. When I take that and light a match to that, it catches on fire. This was a great mystery to the old people. They call it sulfur. So sulfur as a substance has the periphery forces and the condensing forces united. But when I light the match and the sulfur catches on fire, the warmth-levity part of the sulfur goes totally away, and what is left is an ash. If I take the ash, I can't reconstitute the sulfur again because the levity that was present as the sulfur, has gone away. It's called combustion.

In the sal, when I put the salt in the water, it goes away, but when I evaporate the water, it comes back just the same way it was when it went away. The difference is, in sal, the form is retained, but in salt, the form is obliterated. This is a big deal.

So now we get to the phantom. The phantom is the "form template" that the hierarchies use to form the original sense organs that would eventually result in the forming of a body. That's the phantom.

In the creation, there was the idea of a being who would have the experience that they will be a rectifier for the creation. A rectifier is an apparatus in a circuit that keeps the vibrational rates within a certain parameter. So the purpose of creating a being that has sense experience is that it will allow all the different aspects of creation to go through its circuit but stay within a certain parameter. So we get fiat, God the creator creates, and then there's a creation. And the creation was, there will be "beinghood" in this creation. Let's make it a rectifier to the creation and everything will be hunky dory. So a rectifier in a circuit takes random wavelengths and synchronizes them. That's the human.

The human takes wide ranges of wavelengths and brings them into harmony. The function of the human was to have sense organs that brought harmony to the creation. As a rectifier, the human would recognize it and then pass it through the consciousness of those sense organs and then give back to the creation, the rectification, so there wasn't random stuff going on in there – noise. That was the original form of the body of senses for the original being, who would be the rectifier for the creation. That's the role of the human, from Steiner's point of view, to rectify the creation. How? By sensing it. By being present in it and bringing consciousness to it. "This is what the creation looks like." Cool. Let's make a temple and celebrate it.

That's the original form and that form of the energies involved in that rectification, was the original form of what eventually became sensation, which means there's a wave of energy, some type of organ, and it gets rectified and rayed back. That form of the ability to receive and give back and rectify, that's the human phantom.

And that was the original form of the human. But as it evolved, it was understood that, because of the separation of the phantom from the creator, there was going to be a problem for the creator. Now there's this creation running around, sensing with a pattern of "Here's what you're going to sense, here's the music singing in choir." And all the other beings are adding to that and adding to that but it's getting farther and farther away from the original wisdom that formed it. And now it's into this realm down there. So Rudolf Steiner says, in the great wisdom of the cosmos, a portion of the phantom was withheld, while the large part of the phantom went and became all the other human beings. As the wisdom fell into Earth creation, that phantom energy became available for Lucifer and Ahriman because it was the switch, it was the rectifier, it was the focal point that made the creation harmonious.

Grab the energy of the rectifier of the whole cosmos? That's called the fall. So in the fall, the energy of the phantom, the energy of sense experience that is reflecting and harmonizing the creation, was siphoned off and pulled into the realm of Lucifer who caused the phantom to fall into what Rudolf Steiner calls "secretions". The form principle of the substances became manifest substances. They still retain their form principle, as what we now call molecular attraction and repulsion, but they were substantial rather than just energetic. They are still energetic but they are also substantial. Because the sense organs were made of these substances, they became filled with the ash of the fallenness of the form, of the secretion. A secretion is a neurotransmitter. In science a neurotransmitter is a neuro-modulator and a neuro-modulator forms an organ. The sensations that we have of light and sound and color and heat form the organs in the embryo through form activity. It is intelligent because it's highly organized, but it has fallen into secretion. The secretions create the sense organs that give the human sense experience, providing experience that is separate from the creation. So we wake up in our senses but it is "not me". Mom is not me. The Earth is not me. You are not me. My pencil's not me. Only me is me, and sometimes I'm not sure about that.

So the falling of the phantom into secretion created the condition in the sense organs that allowed the human being to separate from the creation, and eventually be in a condition where they would not recognize the creator. They would simply see the creation as a resource.

That's the fall through sensation, and that happened a long time ago as humans began to take the resources of the Earth, the living part of the Earth, and make buildings and aqueducts and vehicles and fires, and God knows what. And then they started killing each other about "the wall of your city is over my territory". That happened back in the very beginning somewhere between the Tigris and the Euphrates, and it's still happening. It's just going to keep happening.

The falling into matter has created in the physical body, a corpse, but the physical body is the invisible body of the forces that are attracting the matter; an alchemical picture. There are many names for that body. Paracelsus called it the Archeus, the archetypal human, the iliaspur, the star body, the America body, the life body, the diamond body. So all these names are for that body of the Son of Man.

All the traditions speak about how we have to actually build organs in that body. We have to construct it through meditative practice in order that we can occupy it, when it hits the fan at the end time. It's not unique to anthroposophy by any means. So that is speaking about the difference between the body of flesh and this body of light. But creation went so far that the sense body became so congealed that it just ended up in wars and turf wars and treasuries and laws, and by the time of Christ, the Romans had spread all over the place. The Jews were fomenting and the hoards were coming out of wherever, and it just had really gotten to be a mess over the issue of the Earth as "just a resource".

So there needed to be something that would come back and say, "You know, that's where the old mysteries have led us – to here." The mysteries of the seven Holy Rishis, the mysteries of Persia and Babylon, the mysteries of Egypt, the Greek mysteries, they all led to this thought. And now the Romans have ripped off and codified and jammed into all the Greek mysteries, as a kind of corpse of all these other mysteries. And there we are.

This is when Christ appears on the stage, and says, "You know, there are new mysteries." But in order to do that, Christ had to be able to hold in a human physical body, the phantom, which is a big deal.

In Steiner's work, I don't want to get into the Jesus children, but there is the possibility in the young Jesus to have a body whose organism operated with the laws of the physical body, but not with the impact of the fall, of not having fallen.

There were secretions, but Rudolf Steiner says that the being who did that was actually an Angel. So the body of Jesus was actually an Angel, and in heaven or in the spiritual world, the Christ gave organs to that Angel to be able to incarnate with the phantom as the operating principle of the life body.

So this was an angelic being in a human body, but the consciousness was kind of spacey, you could say. And then through all kinds of work that was done by Zarathustra, there was an exchange of a higher faculty of consciousness into that being. And then we get

Jesus, growing until the baptism in the Jordan, when that ego that was from Zarathustra was taken away. Because that physical body had been permeated for 30 years by the phantom, the Christ being was able to hold the energy of the Christ. That's a précis of a lot of ideas that Steiner gave. The angelic part of that physical body that was holding the phantom could contain the energy of the I-being of the Christ. That then is the baptism in the Jordan.

Then three years later, after wandering through the world looking for symptoms that the old mysteries contained the answer, He finally had the experience of it not being there. So Steiner gives the picture that Christ Jesus went to his mother, and said, "I don't get it."

And she said to him, "Well, you know, it's really painful for me to tell you this, but it needs you to sacrifice." And that's when He got it. He got his mission, so to speak. It was all there, but He needed the feminine to quicken it. When we finally get to Holy Week, there's this awakening in His Being of this great mission that "I have to die without having fallen. I have to do that for these people around me who couldn't care less for this Earth. They're in my father's house selling doves." Can you imagine?

So that then is the death; it's a ritual death of an innocent being and the phantom is part of that death. Then in the gospels it says, "He gave up the ghost." When He gave up the ghost, He gave up that phantom, and it's that phantom that He took into the Earth to harrow hell.

He placed the phantom into the Earth. The phantom of the physical body in the Earth has no ash. It's just pure salt, meaning it can go into solution without any corpse. That's resurrection. It's a very cool language.

VIII: Easter Sunday

So that's why I thought about the alchemy of Holy Week as a totally alchemical mystery of the salt of the phantom. It comes out of the ash of the unredeemed, fallen physical body, and that is a seed in the center of the Earth that makes the Earth have the potential to become all of that. It's like putting a grain of salt in a supersaturated solution of salt and suddenly the whole thing crystallizes. And what it will crystallize into is the new Sun.

And we humans will be the tenth hierarchy, who will be the spiritual beings who are the monitors and stewards of that Sun. It will be the new Sun of a new cosmos, and we will be the ones who will be the managers of it. We will be the rectifiers of the next round of fallenness, because we will have learned from an Angel through the Christ how to do that.

This is such a beautiful picture that Rudolf Steiner brings of this great mystery of Easter and what it means, and what the potential is. But the difference between that and what we are given by organized religions, is that organized religions say, "He's done it so all you need to do is just sign on the line, and you'll be saved."

But, no, no, no. Rudolf Steiner tells us the message is, "I did it. You need to do it. I just did it as a kind of template of what you need to do." So it's not like the hotline to God. That's the difference. So the book of the new mysteries is not written, because the book is about your life. *That* is the book of the new mysteries.

That's why the Pharisees were unhappy with Him because He was telling the people, "The kingdom is in you." It's not in some book or an authority somewhere. It's in the way you decide to look at the fallenness of your sense life, and how that works. And there's no blame in this at all, because this is a cosmic thing. It's just how much do you wish to suffer?

It's like what Saint Paul said in the letter to the Corinthians: "My strength is made perfect in my weakness." He was preaching in Corinth, a mystery site near Delphi where the ancient priestesses would prophesy. Paul wrote to the Corinthians, *"That even if you speak with the tongues of angels, but you have not love..."* In that letter he says, *Because of the revelations I was receiving, I became exalted. And the Lord sent a messenger of Satan to put a thorn in me, and I asked the Lord three times, "Could you take this from me?" And the Lord said to me, "I am giving you the power to do this if you call me to mind. And you should know that your strength is made perfect in your weakness."*

This is the new mystery: if you don't do it, it's not done. And there's no blame with that. It just means that you go back and sell some doves. Go back to your business, go back to your fields, that's OK. But it's not getting the work done.

Exercise: The Gate of the Sun and Moon

There is a little meditation that comes from an alchemical source shown in the figure below.

This meditation is to try to understand this issue of the phantom, and the placing of the phantom in the Earth, and the future. It's called "the gate of the Sun and Moon", and some of you know it. I'll explain how it works.

In the figure below, you can see a thing that looks a bit like an orange; that's the Earth. The Moon is rotating counterclockwise around the Earth. Then there's a little human figure, and that is you.

VIII: Easter Sunday

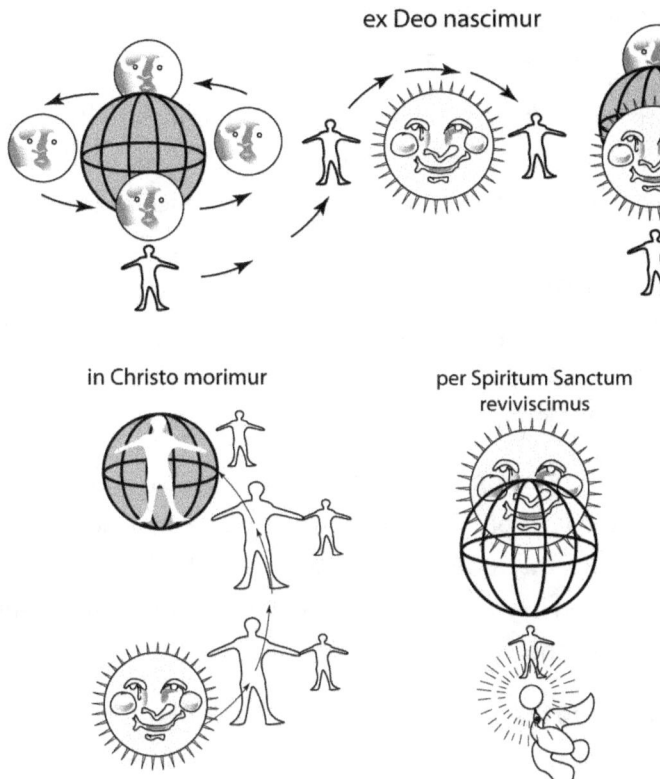

You imagine the Earth. Then you move above the Earth and look down on the Earth, and then look out towards the rising Sun in the east. Then you try to remember where the Moon is. If the Moon is full, that's on the opposite side from the Sun. If the Moon is dark, it's on the same side of the Sun, and that's what you see in the diagram. You see the Earth, and the Moon going around the Earth. There's a little man looking at the Moon going around the Earth and to the right is the Sun.

In alchemy, there is a gate between the Sun and the Moon. You can learn to enter time consciously so that the elemental beings who move the planets, the spirits of the rotation of time, give to you a presentment of the qualities of time.

But in order to do that, you have to get away from Earth time and understand that Earth time is a huge convention. Get off the grid, so to speak. So this is an exercise to lift your consciousness to the spot where you participate in the movement of time imaginatively, in such a way that you can replicate this drama that I just described of the phantom being brought from the Sun, brought down to the Earth and placed there, and then the future. This is called the gate of the Sun and Moon.

So you imagine looking at the Earth and you try to imagine where the Moon is in its orbit. That means you may have to learn a little astronomy, but that doesn't hurt your brain at all. You imagine where the Moon is; you picture that. And if the Moon is to the left, that is the full Moon. That gate is wide open.

If the Moon is to the right, it's on the same side of the Earth as the Sun, but there's still a space between them. So you imagine that you move away from the Earth and go between the Moon and the Sun. Wherever the Moon is, it'll be on your left and the Sun will be on your right. Just organize space that way, so as you do the exercise, you move through. Then imagine that you turn to your right and go behind the Sun. That's what you see in the diagram. The little man moves from looking at the Earth and the Moon, moves between the Moon and the Sun, and then goes around the Sun. On the right, you see the little man down below, the Sun and the Earth and the Moon beyond.

Imagine yourself behind the Sun, looking at the relationship between the Earth and the Moon. In that position, you look up and

VIII: Easter Sunday

around, and see the whole heavens with this drama of the Earth and the Sun and the Moon in front of you. Now, I'll go back to the first thing I read to you from Rudolf Steiner's *Christ and the Spiritual World*: *The working together of thinking, feeling and willing has to be kept in order. Not, however, from all the planets, but only through the Sun, Moon, and Earth, so that through the interworking of the Sun, Moon, and Earth, if this is harmonious and is made fit for the harmonious cooperation of his three soul powers, this engenders the Virgin Sophia.*

So we're actually taking the Sun and the Moon and the Earth as teachers of this process, in our imagination. But it's not a random imagination because it's based on the actual positions of the Sun and the Moon and the Earth. I have to do a little research to find out where that is.

Go through the gate of the Sun and the Moon, I turn, I look at the Sun and then the Earth and the Moon, wherever that is, and then I look in my imagination, I see all the starry realms behind it. I realize that the Sun, Moon and Earth are actually the source of my soul.

I look at the starry heaven of all creation and in my soul, I imagine saying the great Rosicrucian mantra, *ex Deo nascimur*, out of God we are being born. I'm putting myself in the consciousness of the ordering of the creation from the whole realm of the zodiac into the realm of the Earth and then the Sun, so I can understand what is the role of my soul in this. *Ex Deo nascere*, out of God we are continually being born, nascere: to be born. That is step one.

Then I imagine that there is a great being who emerges from the Sun. Rudolf Steiner gives the picture that Christ was the being of the Sun who was revered in the ancient times. He was the great Sun Being, the Christ. But in order for the mystery of the redemption to happen, the Sun Being had to actually come to Earth, live in a body of flesh, die in a body of flesh, and then become one with the spirit of the Earth. So we imagine a great being coming from the Sun, and you see the great being and the small being are holding hands there. You follow the Sun Being down and you go behind the Earth so that the Earth covers the Sun. When you are in that position, you are in what is known as the Spiritual Sun. The actual Sun, that we see with our senses, has fallen.

So when I see the Earth blot out that Sun, and I follow the Sun Being through Golgotha down into the Earth, through the harrowing of hell and placing a seed of a new Sun in the center of the dark Earth. And then the inner mantra is, *in Christo morimur,* in Christ we are dying; we are dying, along with the Christ into the Earth. When you give up the ghost, you take your vehicle and give it back to the Earth.

In Christo morimur is: I watch Christ die into the Earth as an imagination of what my soul has to experience, incarnating again and again, and watching myself die. Each time I do, there's a kind of a lesson learned there, "I thought it was the end of me, but now I see I'm going to have to come back and deal with the person I disrespected last time, and my other actions." So there we start to see karma.

In Christo morimur. I watch Christ as the Sun Being go into the Earth and place in the inner core of the Earth, a seed of light of a Sun. So there I am, in the darkness, and that seed of light is the seed of the phantom that is the seed of human development of their senses, to the point where they can release their senses from the bondage of matter. This is just total alchemy: it is my consciousness that changes matter. It's about consciousness.

That seed is the potential of humans to find in their sense experience the original form of the phantom, so that their consciousness frees itself up from ash, and becomes more like the salt of a new world, the seed of a new world through sensation. I watch as humans do that, the seed of light in the dark Earth begins to make the dark Earth transparent, because matter is being sublimated by human imagination. I watch as the Earth becomes more transparent, the old Sun starts to shine through the Earth with a new blood, filled with light. That new blood, filled with light, permeates the Earth, and as the Earth begins to become lighter and rosier – the rosy light of the new Sun arising – it gives me a perception that even though I'm on the dark side, something that I am doing has something to do with what I'm looking at. Something that I am bringing to this, has something to do with the way the Earth is changing. This is climate change. Something you are doing has something to do with the way the Earth is changing. It's just the tip of the iceberg for that one.

As we become more aware of the fact that the Earth is vulnerable to humans, to human activity, the Earth will start to become treated more in a sacred manner because we'll realize it's not a resource, it's a being. It's a living being and its consciousness includes us, our consciousness, because we will be the stewards of the new Sun. But we need to understand that that action is through the Holy Spirit. So that is what is in the third part of the diagram. You see the Sun shining through the Earth. The Earth actually becomes the Sun. Humans will observe it, but then behind them, in the spiritual Sun, in the darkness, they have a perception that there is a being there of the Holy Spirit, who is shining on their Sophianic effort to lift to wisdom. Rudolf Steiner says that Sophia will be overshadowed by the Holy Spirit and released from Lucifer's prison of lies, through our activity.

We will lift human wisdom back into holy wisdom. Late and slow, but it's in the program. When that happens, in the new Sun, we will have the experience of redeeming Sophia and, in a very unusual turn of events, Rudolf Steiner said, Lucifer becomes the Holy Spirit. Lucifer will be purged of his pride by our effort to redeem fallenness that he has put into our sensation.

Ahriman will receive the ash that we push out of the creation to make a little seed of evil, to allow the weakness to be perfected into strength in the new universe.

This is really out there. It's a beautiful thing. This is in Steiner's work, but it's in pieces all over the place. Steiner was bringing it in through inspiration, but now we have all the books and we just have to use thinking to pull it out. Otherwise, it just becomes sheet music, just singing in the choir even though you don't get it.

It's OK to not get it, but it's better to try to get it, isn't it? You feel a lot stupider when you try to get it, but your wisdom will be perfected in your ignorance.

This meditation comes out of my questioning for years: What is Christ in the etheric? And what is the human phantom? For years, I tried to understand that. I looked at Goethe and I looked at Steiner. There is a lot written about the etheric by other writers and in science, but it is actually a theological question.

And it really has to do with this problem of fundamentalism. I can't say it often enough that fundamentalism simply means, "I have my opinion and it's more correct than yours." So I form a judgment of you, even though I have no idea what's going on, and I put that judgment out on you unconsciously, to scratch an itch that I have, about how I don't feel good about something I'm doing, something that I'm not sure about and it's exacerbated and amplified by the media. So the human soul has this great power in it, of the phantom, the seed of the phantom to be able to change, to tell the mountain to get up and go jump in the lake. That's our birthright given to us through the deed of Christ on Golgotha, and through the resurrection. The resurrection proved that the phantom lives and that the phantom is in us. Rudolf Steiner is very clear: other people came back from the dead, but only one person came back from the dead through the action of the phantom, because all the other people who came back from the dead, you don't have the Old Testament saying that they were going to do it.

The Old Testament was always pointing to this deed, and the stories of Osiris and Orpheus, and all the pictures of these beings that have to come down and go into a cave and get trashed, and then come back again. They are all Christ pictures of this deed: the deed to come back and be in a body and die in a body, but the only place I've ever experienced the rationale for the phantom is in the work of Rudolf Steiner, and with that imagination, Holy Week makes so much more sense. Yes, this actually is the redemption. So that's why I brought to you the Gnostic gospels and this picture of Pistis Sophia, because they were all talking about this problem. But it's true, the genius of Rudolf Steiner is that he named it, and said that this is the work that Christ did: to bring the phantom, to put the phantom into the seed in the center of the Earth where the magicians are working, so that humans can then redeem the Earth as the spirit of Christ.

Alchemy of Holy Week

VIII: Easter Sunday

References

Alchemical Wedding of Christian Rosenkreutz

The Fall of the Spirits of Darkness by Rudolf Steiner

Pistis Sophia Coptic Codex

Christ and the Spiritual World by Rudolf Steiner

The Three Years by Emil Bock

The Inner Life of the Earth by Rudolf Steiner

For those engaged with Spirit

This workshop is also available as an audio series at
dennisklocek.com/lecture/the-alchemy-of-holy-week

Also by Dennis Klocek

Sacred Agriculture
The Harmonies of Storms
Climate: Soul of the Earth
The Seers Handboook
Weather and Cosmos
Drawing From the Book of Nature
and more.

See dennisklocek.com for

Audio Lectures
Video Courses
Articles
Publications